Fiddle and Fight

*Russell Brodine playing his Michelangelo Nardelli
bass with a bow he made.*

Fiddle and Fight

by
Russell V. Brodine

with

Virginia Warner Brodine

International Publishers
New York

Cover Illustration by Cecelia Corr
Cover Design by Peter Frazier
"Committees and Such" and the material in the appendix were published in
Senza Sordino, Vol. 39, No. 1 (January 2001).
Cover photo and photos, pp. 168-169: Janine Shinkoskey Brodine
News article, p. 108: *St. Louis Post-Dispatch*
Photo, p. 126: *St. Louis Post-Dispatch*/reprinted with permission
Editorial catoons, pp. 136 and 139: © Engelhardt in the *St. Louis Post-Dispatch*/reprinted with permission
Appendix: reprinted with permission of the St. Louis Sypmphony Musicians' Council

Printed in Canada

Library of Congress Cataloging-in-Publication Data

Brodine, Russell V. (Russell Victor), 1912-
  Fiddle and fight / by Russell V. Brodine with Virginia Warner Brodine.--1st ed.
     p. cm.
  Includes bibliographical references (p.) and index.
  ISBN 0-7178-0729-0 (ppk.: alk. paper)
    1. Brodine, Russell V. (Russell Victor), 1912- 2. Double bassists--United States--
Biography. 3. Orchestral musicians--Labor unions--Organizing--
United States. I. Brodine, Virginia. II. Title.

  ML418.B695 A3 2001
  787.5'092--dc21
  [B]

                                                              2001024334

Dedication

Forever (or even beyond) I shall be thankful to
Virginia, Cynthia and Marc for their arduous
efforts in turning these thoughts into book form.

Table of Contents

Illustrations

A Life Lived With Music

This is the story of my forty-three years in music. Not as a musical star—that is exactly the point. I am proud of having played many good, low, rich notes on my double bass. For the most part, I did so as part of a bass section that was part of a symphony orchestra. I was not a virtuoso.

Our society makes much of individuals, of stars, of celebrities. Nevertheless, not only in music but in every sphere of our life, almost everything worthwhile is created by the work of people who are never in the limelight, who are important because they work together.

The same thing is true of change and progress. It comes about in the main not because of great leaders, but because people work together to bring about that change. Why do I call this story "Fiddle and Fight"? When I started as a professional musician, this was the situation: After practicing throughout our youth, avoiding rough and tumble activity to protect our fingers, taking music lessons and studying at conservatories, musicians auditioned and got a symphony position—with a salary of less than $2,000 a year. We *needed* to fight.

My life is one small piece of musical/social/political history. It is incomplete without the stories of other men and women who worked for the advancement of music and musicians in our society and for changes in that society for the benefit of all working people. I am proud to have been part of that struggle. It has had its ups and downs, but both music and society are better for it.

Struggles similar to ours took place in other orchestras. Some of the people who played important parts are already gone, such as Fred Batchelder of Philadelphia, a string bass player and my roommate during my last year at the Curtis Institute of Music. George Zazofsky of the Boston Symphony, a violinist and the first president of the International Conference of Symphony and Opera Musicians, was another Curtis acquaintance.

There are many, many such people. Sometimes they are unaccustomed to writing and may not have the skill. I am fortunate in having had a writer/editor in the family. Every family should have one! This book is just one of the many things Virginia and I worked on together during our fifty-eight year marriage. Several of the friends and colleagues who were with me in St. Louis also helped to shape this book with advice, remembrances, and corrections.

A few words on Virginia's work on this short opus: She and I engaged in a controversy regarding the authorship. She won! I wanted her name to be listed as co-author. A cover that says "by Russell V. Brodine *with* Virginia Warner Brodine," is inadequate but must remain because she insisted on that formulation. I truly believe that although she was not a musician, in this instance as well as in many orchestra struggles, Virginia played a crucial role with her writing talent. When we packed up to leave St. Louis, I was about to dispose of the large box of agendas, programs, notes, letters and articles pertaining to the

Virginia Warner Brodine

years of our work. Emphatically she exclaimed, "No! That's history!" Thus, "with" understates her importance to the project!

She is no longer here; my wife of 58 years died of cancer, May 12, 2000.

One person who does have the skill and has written about some of these matters is Edward Arian, who left the bass section of the Philadelphia Orchestra after twenty years to become a political scientist. His book is *Bach, Beethoven and Bureaucracy, the Case of the Philadelphia Orchestra.*[1]

History is not only what happened yesterday. Today's musicians are now making the history of their profession and their union and are part of the ongoing story of culture in this country. These struggles are important. Without struggle, there is no progress. Without an understanding of past struggles, new ones must back up and start over.

This book is for the younger musicians who picked up where I left off or who are just entering the profession and need to know where it has been so they can chart where it is going.

It is also for members of symphony audiences everywhere. It will give them a glimpse backstage.

And it is for my comrades and my union sisters and brothers who were making history onstage and offstage, on assembly lines and picket lines, in hundreds of different occupations long before my part in it began, and who will continue to do so long after I am gone.

SPRING HILL

My career as a professional musician began during my senior year in high school when I was eighteen. The Seattle Repertory Theater under Florence Bean James and her husband, Burton ("Pop") James, was preparing a production of *Peer Gynt*. They hired a small orchestra. I was to be the bass player.

Grieg's *Peer Gynt Suite* was familiar to me because our high school orchestra had played it, but I got the music and practiced assiduously. When the time came for the first rehearsal I went to my brother's apartment where I had left my bass.

To my great consternation, no one was home and the doors were locked. I felt that my whole career rested on my ability to make this rehearsal, so I broke in, picked up my instrument and reported for work. I knew I would hear from Franz later about breaking into his place but considered any sacrifice on my part (or his) well worth it.

I enjoyed the performances. There were never any more decent bosses than the Jameses. Their theater played an important role in Seattle's cultural life until they were redbaited and driven out of town and out of the country in the McCarthyite hysteria of the 1950s. Our loss was Canada's gain.

At the time of the Peer Gynt job I joined the union. This, too, made me feel that I was on my way as a professional musician. I knew that all workers needed unions, and I was now a worker. So I became a member of Local 76 of the American Federation of Musicians and have been a member of the AFM ever since—more than 70 years.

My story actually begins much earlier. Like so many stories in this country, it begins with the arrival of immigrants.

Sigrid Sophia Tingstrom, a young woman of twenty-two from a family of Swedish coppersmiths, arrived in the United States on January 1, 1900. Like her older brother, Axel Leandro, who had preceded her, she headed for Minnesota. For the next few years she worked as a domestic while she learned the language and gained some familiarity with the new country. A photograph of the time shows that she was a slender, attractive young woman. Unlike the stereotype of the Scandinavian, but like many Swedes, she had brown hair and eyes.

In 1903 she married Franz H. Brodine, also of Swedish birth. He was a widowed piano teacher with an infant son. He had fled Sweden to avoid the draft. These were my parents. They moved to Washington State soon after their marriage and a few years later settled on Spring Hill, a semi-rural area at the edge of Spokane.

The baby David was just the first in a large family. Mother bore one child after another until we were eight. After naming the first two children after themselves, Franz and Sigrid, they named the other three boys for French and English philosophers: Voltaire, (Herbert) Russell and (Herbert) Spencer, the other two girls for characters from Shakespeare: Juliet and Cecelia.

My middle name is Victor after the socialist leader, Eugene Victor Debs, who was running for president in 1912, the year I was born. I was one of many children named after Debs, for he was held in high esteem in the early years of the century. He garnered a million votes and later went to jail for his opposition to World War I.

Both his name and the influence of his ideas surfaced many years later when a group of about ten people from around Central Washington gathered to discuss the issue of peace in the election of 1984. A man named Gene told us that he, too, had been named for Debs, and a younger woman said her father, Eugene, was another Debs namesake.

For fourteen years after her marriage, my mother was always either pregnant or caring for an infant, usually both. At the same time, she held the family together and managed its daily life with the meager income my father earned as a piano teacher.

One of the most important pieces of furniture in our house was the big black kitchen range, with a wood box beside it, where Mother cooked for her hungry brood. Rivaling it in importance was the piano in the living room where Father taught his pupils. When he was giving a lesson we had to be quiet, which was difficult for a lively bunch like us.

Sometimes he went to the homes of his students instead. When I watched him walk off down the road I was proud of this impressive looking Music Professor. He carried himself well, dressed well, and had a full beard, which was not common in those days.

However, I was always glad to see him go. He was a petty tyrant, always scolding one of us. We could hear him at night after all of us were in bed, yelling at my mother. Sometimes the older girls would send little Cecelia to ask him to let us go to sleep. Being the smallest, she was the only one who could do so without inviting retaliation.

Our father did not usually abuse us physically, although my older brothers remember some severe beatings. If I saw him coming when I was playing in the schoolyard, I would run to the other side of the building to avoid a scolding in the presence of my schoolmates.

West Euclid Avenue, where we lived, was not much more than a lane, intersecting the gravel County Road that came up Spring Hill from the city and ran off north across the plateau. There was one house across Euclid from us, on the edge of the hill, but few other houses. The Brodine family simply expanded its activities behind our house and on both sides with no regard for property lines.

In back of our house, barn, and woodshed was a flat, fertile piece of ground, watered by the spring that gave the hill its name. There we had our garden. As we also kept a cow, we had plenty of manure for fertilizer.

The vegetables were delicious. I liked to pull up carrots, peel off all but the heart, eat that and discard the rest. Or I would sit in the pea patch, shelling fresh peas into my mouth.

When there were extra vegetables, we peddled them in town. We had one of the wagons that were standard playthings for children in those days. We built up the sides so we could pile it high with corn, beans, peas, and squash. This was the way we earned the money to pay for our school clothes. On the way home with an empty wagon we would squander ten or fifteen cents at the bakery for a bag of broken cookies.

Long before the present fad for oats, oatmeal was a principal item in our diet simply because it was one of the cheapest foods available.

We developed habits of scrounging, reusing, and recycling as poor people did out of necessity. Even in more prosperous times I have continued these habits, now also as a matter of ecological principle. Scroungers of the world, unite! You have nothing to lose but pollution!

One day our father came hurrying in, calling out, "Every-body come. Bring tubs and buckets. Don't ask questions. Hurry! Hurry!"

We followed him to the County Road, where a truck carrying a load of navy beans had lost a catch on its tailgate and spread a sheet of beans all over the road. We set to work picking them up and filling our buckets.

When a wagon or a car came up the road, we shouted, "Don't crush the beans!" This became a byword in our family. When we wanted to warn one another of impending disaster we would shout (or whisper) "Don't crush the beans."

We ate baked beans once a week for years, seasoned with a little gravel.

I once told this story to a group of colleagues. The only one who really appreciated it was Alfred Genovese, an oboe player who had grown up in a poor Italian family in one of the eastern cities. Years later, when I was in New York on tour and Genovese was playing in the Metropolitan Opera Orchestra, we encountered each other on the street, and he saluted me with a shout: "Don't crush the beans!"

Wood heated our house on Spring Hill and fired our cook stove. It took a woodshed bigger than most present-day garages to hold enough for the winter. We cut down pine trees on the hill, brought the logs home, cut, split and stacked the wood.

In spite of the chores, we had plenty of time to play in the woods and down by the Spokane River. We frequented the golf course, hunting lost golf balls. (Any ball that had stopped rolling was "lost.")

During wet weather we liked to dam up a creek, laboring over it and calling it "good work for the government." All this outdoor freedom made us carefree and independent and was a welcome escape from tensions at home.

There was little demonstrative affection in our family, but I developed a strong tie to my mother, and we children became a close-knit tribe. There were few other children nearby so we worked and played together. Of course there were squabbles. For instance, the "big kids" scorned the "little kids" and sometimes barred them from games. In the main, though, we hung together and developed a Children's Mutual Protective Association against our father.

Although we resented him, we had him to thank for introducing us to music. We grew up loving it. We heard some of the great singers—Galla Curci, Caruso—on a windup phonograph. Listening to music made my spine tingle and gave me goose bumps. I knew that making music would be the best thing, the only possible thing, for me to do with my life.

Our parents were also responsible for our early exposure to radical thought. Neither of them bought into the World War I slogan of "a war to end war." This made them unpatriotic in the eyes of others, but they stuck to their beliefs.

Like many immigrant parents, ours were eager for their children to be as American as possible. We learned little of our Swedish heritage or language. One Swedish friend who came to the house gave us a taste of it, lovingly reciting Swedish poetry and stories. This old man was a self-educated street sweeper with an encyclopedic memory. He loved English literature as well as Swedish and could recite Shakespeare by the page. He composed his own poetry as he pushed his cart through the streets, cleaning up after the horses.

Our parents decided on a move to Seattle in 1924. The University of Washington was one of the magnets. David, my half-

The Brodine Family enroute from Spokane to Seattle in 1924. L to R: Franz, Father, Voltaire, Mother, Juliet, Sigrid, Spencer, Cecilia. Russell above the crowd. The two men at right were friendly strangers.

brother, had run away to California, but the other older children were in their teens and would soon be ready for college.

Our furniture was shipped on the train and all nine of us piled into our Model T Ford. Our father had acquired this car a year or two earlier but never learned to drive, so Franz, as the oldest boy, was at the wheel.

The route was longer than it is on today's freeways, the roads unpaved. In the mountain passes, the car could not pull the heavy load, so most of us had to walk up the last steep grades. A Good Samaritan lightened the load by giving Voltaire and me a lift in his Model T. As he picked up speed and left the family car behind I got scared, thinking we were being kidnapped.

We arrived safely in Seattle and before long were settled in a house near Greenlake.

BASS NOTES

We no longer had all of Spring Hill for roaming, but we had the lake to replace it. Uncle Axel gave us a canoe, and we developed expertise at handling it. We fished, swam, and paddled. Voltaire and I played checkers sitting in the bottom of the canoe. Our checkers were homemade pegs and would not slide on the board even if the water became a little rough. When the wind had carried us across the lake, we would paddle back, resume the game, and drift again.

When our father had to go across the lake to give a lesson, we paddled him across and came back to take him home. He was now getting a dollar and a half for each lesson, up from the dollar he had received in Spokane.

Our family continued to go to meetings around various issues. While in Spokane I could enjoy only the fun and food at the radical picnics; I was not old enough to understand the content of the speeches or to get my first lessons in the importance of cooperation in the political arena.

I remember more than one rally to "Free Mooney and Billings." They were active trade unionists and socialists framed on a murder charge in 1916 after a bomb exploded in a "Preparedness Day" parade in San Francisco (preparedness for World War I). They were finally released by Governor Olson of California in 1933 after seventeen years of suffering.

Another case of class injustice that had a profound effect on me, as on many other people, was the trial and execution of Nicola Sacco and Bartolomeo Vanzetti in 1927. They were anarchists convicted ostensibly for a robbery and murder but actually for their radical activity. There were demonstrations on their behalf throughout this country and the world. I was fifteen at the time, and while fearful of being clubbed by the cops, I took part in a student demonstration organized by my brother Franz. We carried handmade signs and marched down Westlake Boulevard to the *Seattle Times* building.

The big difference for us in our new home was that now we not only listened to music and studied it but also began to perform it. Franz and Sigrid had become quite proficient on the violin. Voltaire and Cecelia took piano lessons from our old man and learned to play the harp as well.

My father brought home a cello, which was to be for me. The whole family circled around to admire the new instrument. He stood it up in front of me, then took it away, saying, "No, you're too small," and gave it to Juliet instead. The kid who was too small was soon bigger than Juliet and had to carry the cello all over town for her.

Meanwhile, I got a violin. Although I had several lessons from a professional, Franz was generally my teacher. He would take me up to his room, put a piece of music on the stand, say "Practice!" then lie down and go to sleep. Needless to say, I did not advance rapidly.

Along with the others, though, I played in our family orchestra. We performed in churches, at radical meetings, and once for a Chinese festival. When I got to Lincoln High School, I played viola in the school orchestra.

Our father's ambition was to make professional musicians of us all. One day he met Carl Pitzer, the Lincoln High music teacher, on the street and was congratulated on his talented children. According to Mr. Pitzer, all of us could do well in the profession "except Russell."

When I heard that, it was a blow. I worshipped Mr. Pitzer, who was an excellent teacher and a talented director. Yet I was not willing to accept his judgment. I was determined to make music my life. I was well aware of the inadequacy of my contribution to the orchestra as a viola player—I did not even have a true viola, only a made-over violin. However, an opportunity to try another instrument arose. The school orchestra needed a string bass player. I borrowed the school instrument during the summer vacation, took it home, set up my music stand in the garage and the whole summer between my freshman and sophomore years, I nearly worked my butt off. It was a turning point in my life. This was the instrument that was right for me.

What attracted me to the bass and to orchestral music? Certainly not the pay, which in those days was not enough to live on even in the major orchestras. I loved music and wanted to be part of making it.

There was something else, too. The bass is not a solo instrument, but it is a fundamental part of the cooperation that makes orchestral music great. I am both a music buff and a cooperation buff. As an orchestral musician, I would be part of that superb cooperative production, one in a section of five to ten basses, in an orchestra of eighty to more than a hundred musicians. On a more intimate scale, I would be the only bass in a quintet or chamber orchestra.

My bass playing in the school orchestra changed Mr. Pitzer's estimation of my ability. He helped me in any way he could to prepare for a career in music. I was selected as one of fourteen bass players from around the state for an All-State High School Orchestra. We went to Spokane for three days of training and a concert.

Now that I had begun to show promise on the bass, my father arranged for me to have private lessons from Herman Evers, principal bass in the Seattle Symphony.

The following summer, with Pitzer's help, I was one of two Seattle students to receive scholarships for eight weeks of study at Interlochen, the national high school music camp in Michigan, then in the second year of its existence. I even got my picture in the daily paper.

That was a musical thrill for me: eight weeks of concentrated study, private lessons from Alex Trempeneau, a bassist from the Cincinnati Symphony, and rehearsals in an or-

TWO SEATTLE HIGH SCHOOL MUSICIANS ARE HONORED

Helen Fenton, Broadway, and Russel Brodine, Lincoln, awarded 8-week training courses in National High School Orchestra at Interlochen, Mich. —*Times Photos*

chestra with other instrumentalists. Many of the others had much more training than I and some seemed to me to be accomplished musicians already.

It was an important experience in another way. It was the first time I had ever been away from home. The train trip to Chicago and from there up to Michigan carried me what seemed an immense distance from my family. Together with the eight weeks in a beautiful setting entirely among people who were total strangers, it helped me to grow up.

I came home, happy to be back and full of my experiences. My father's greeting was, "Voltaire is fixing the roof. Change your clothes and get up there and work. You're no better than anybody else."

In my senior year, I taught bass to other students at Lincoln and in several other high schools. The experience was important for the development of my mastery of the instrument and my self-confidence but not for the remuneration. I received 35 cents for each lesson and had to pay 20 cents on the streetcar to go back and forth to the other schools.

By this time, Sigrid had graduated from the University and was teaching music in an Oregon high school. Franz and Juliet were playing in the University orchestra. I filled in there when a bass was needed and got additional encouragement from the director, Walter Welke.

The music teacher at West Seattle High School arranged for a radio concert presenting one movement of Schubert's quintet in A-major, *The Trout*. He took the piano part, assembled others to play violin, viola and cello and asked me to join them.

This Schubert work, by that most melodic of composers, is a gem of the chamber music literature, just as his *Unfinished Symphony* is a melodic gem of symphonic literature. The quintet gets its name from the folk song *Die Forellen*, which Schubert used for the theme of one movement.

I don't know of any other piece of chamber music with such an important and rewarding part for the bass. This was the first of many performances of *The Trout* in which I participated. It wove itself into my musical and my political life, as most of the later performances were for causes to which I was committed.

Ironically for the father who tried so hard to make musicians of us, the more proficient we became, the less respect we had for him musically. We could now see that he could perform only one showy piece and had no repertoire beyond it. He professed to be a professor but wasn't. He claimed to have studied under the great pianists of his day but hadn't. He boasted that he could get a good student an "international scholarship," but there was no such thing. He was neither a good pianist nor a good teacher.

He was more difficult than ever to live with and even his outer shell, which had impressed me so much as a child, was deteriorating, as he no longer kept up his appearance.

With even her youngest child, Spencer, in high school and the older ones working, our mother no longer had to be tied to her unhappy marriage. With her children urging her on, she filed for divorce. We closed the door of the house against our father.

David, who was married and back from California, took him in for a while. Without his family, he rapidly went downhill both psychologically and economically. He wound up in a Hooverville, one of those shantytowns thrown up during the depression by the unemployed, and there he died.

Sadly, we could not mourn him. His children resented him, even hated him, but in later years I recognized that psychological problems were at the root of his failures as a husband and father, and I no longer felt bitter.

During my last year in high school I joined the union and got that first professional job, playing in fifty performances of *Peer Gynt* at the Seattle Repertory Theater.

After my graduation, my teacher, Mr. Evers, arranged for me to participate in Seattle Symphony rehearsals. He was an old German who didn't communicate too clearly. I understood that this meant I was to be a member of the Symphony. I was in seventh heaven. When I was informed that I was just there to rehearse, I came down from heaven with a thump.

Wanting no part of being a second-class musician, I refused to rehearse unless I could also play the concerts. This was my first successful revolt. I was accepted as a member of the bass section beginning with the 1931-32 season.

It could hardly be called a season. The depression hit symphonies hard, and the already short Seattle season had been reduced from nine subscription concerts to six, children's concerts from ten to five with five pop concerts.[2]

My pay was $22.50 a week. In order to make a living, some members of the symphony had formerly played in the movie theaters, but their jobs were disappearing as the "talkies" with their recorded music replaced silent films. Many symphony musicians were teachers; others found jobs not related to music, but just when the theater jobs were disappearing, the depression hit, making it hard to find any kind of work.[3]

Seattle Symphony on tour in front of the Mormon Tabernacle in Salt Lake City. Russell is fifth from the right in the front row.

One of the numbers programmed for the symphony that season was Debussy's *The Afternoon of a Faun.* I had never heard of it and could make no sense of it. I was convinced that it was too modern to last!

The symphony checks and the little I could earn teaching added up to a very small income. I continued to live at home and turned my checks over to Mother, keeping just enough for carfare and lunch.

Although I now considered myself a professional musician, much more training was necessary if I were ever to be accepted into one of the major orchestras. Carl Pitzer told me about the Curtis Institute of Music in Philadelphia, an all-scholarship conservatory. Some of its students were even given additional financial help.

My letter of application to Curtis was for

Seattle Symphony on tour in the Cascade Mountains

myself and all my brothers and sisters, indicating that all of us would need such extra help. I doubt if the school ever received another application quite like that.

The reply informed me that applicants were required to audition in Philadelphia. Franz was now earning a living as a jazz musician and was not focused on a symphony career as I was, but he was willing to audition for Curtis, too.

He had a Model A Ford roadster with a rumble seat that would go as fast as thirty-five miles an hour. In the spring of 1932, the two of us and Laurence Gustafson, a friend who played flute, drove across the country, taking turns at the wheel, driving day and night. Farmers were hard hit by the depression, and all across the Midwest eggs were our principal food at six to ten cents a dozen.

Franz and Russell in the Model A Ford. Russell usually rode in the rumble seat.

Whenever we approached a tollgate, I would get into the rumble seat and close the top down so we would have less toll to pay. One tollgate keeper hitched a ride with us as we left the gate. Not being able to hear the conversation, I could not understand why I was still shut in and yelled, "Hey, let me out!" Our passenger merely admonished us not to do that again.

When we arrived in Philadelphia, we looked for a place to

Russell assumes the position

camp. We pitched our tent in what appeared to be a park and prepared to sleep. We were routed out by the police, who informed us that we were camping on a mainline estate. They kindly conducted us to Fairmont Park where we camped as long as we were in the city.

My audition was successful, but only mine. Not that Franz and Gus were less proficient than I was, but Curtis had fewer applicants on bass

Russell and Franz at breakfast

than on violin or flute, so I had less competition. I was on Cloud Nine. I would enter Curtis in the fall.

We returned to Seattle. That summer my brothers and I were musicians on the President liners to China, Japan and the Philippines. We were paid only a dollar a day, but we had a glimpse of those countries, so different from our own. Although our job was to entertain the passengers, our papers described us, like other workers on the ships, as "able bodied seamen."

We had a few days off in China, giving us an opportunity to see a little more than the ports. My respect and liking for the Chinese people grew. I especially enjoyed their sense of humor. In spite of the language barrier, we shared many laughs. Their poverty was appalling. People were sleeping in the streets (as

Russell roughing it

they are doing now in U.S. cities). Small children workers slept under their workbenches.

When on board, we ate with the passengers, rather than with the crew, but we did even better than that. We made friends with the pantry man and helped him juggle his heavy boxes. The captain and first mate didn't get much of their guava jelly and cream cheese while we were aboard.

The brothers in Shanghai—Voltaire, Franz, Russell

Back in the U.S.A., the fall school year was coming, and with it came the problem of how to get to Philadelphia. No money, no Ford, and three thousand miles to go. I chose the boxcars. It was pretty rough, and I almost gave up before I was well started, but my fellow travelers knew the ropes and helped me along.

Traveling across the northern states in September, I saw the Aurora Borealis for the first time from the top of a boxcar. It was very cold and windy up there. Despite the cold, a divinity student, on his way to school like me, went to sleep so soundly that he began to turn over as if he were home in bed. He would have rolled right off the moving car. I caught him just in time.

On another night, another rider and I opened a kind of trap door in a refrigerator car and crawled inside. One end of the car was full of ice; the rest held cherries from the Yakima Valley. We lay down on the ice, smelling those cherries but unable to get to them. It was less cold than being outside in the wind but hardly warm enough to go to sleep, so we talked all night. My companion was headed back home to Iceland. He was a Communist and was disgusted with the depression conditions in the U.S. When we parted a few days later, he gave me his overcoat.

As we approached Minneapolis, I was told to watch out for a yard bull (a railroad company cop) wearing a "cork hat," the kind usually thought of as a tropical helmet. He had the reputation of being tough on bums and had even been known to shoot them. Sneaking around the end of a car in the Minneapolis rail yard, I ran right into his arms.

"Hey, where you going, kid?"

"To school in Philadelphia."

"Your train will leave in about an hour. Just stay to hell out of my way."

It was an adventurous trip but not an experience I wanted to repeat. Going back and forth to school for the next few years, I hitchhiked, resting half way across in Minneapolis, with my Aunt Matilda.

STUDENT YEARS IN PHILADELPHIA

In the autumn of 1932, the depression hit its third year and its hard bottom. To be a student or a young worker—and I was both—meant a constant struggle to stay alive. It was more the optimism of youth than the reality of the economic situation that kept me focused on a musical career.

Not long after I arrived in Philadelphia, I picked up a leaflet calling for a demonstration for more relief, more food for the city's hungry families. Preoccupied with where my own next meal was coming from, I read it with personal as well as political interest.

The demonstration took place at Philadelphia's City Hall, presided over by a statue of the great Quaker, William Penn. The dingy building, its stones blackened by years of smoke and grime, was in the process of being cleaned. Scaffolds were erected against the walls. On part of the façade, the original yellow color now shown forth, clean and bright.

The vibrant voice of Russell Watson, a handsome young African-American, rang out, "They're cleaning the outside. Let's clean the inside!"

The crowd surged forward but found the iron gates across the doors closed against us. A call was heard: "All able seamen up forward!"

It was really a general call for those with physical strength, but being (on paper at least) an able seaman, I obediently went forward and found myself, a skinny music student, in the shock troop of big, brawny, work-hardened guys whose job was to break through the gates. It is doubtful if my strength added much to the successful effort, from which I emerged breathless and with a torn jacket.

We made our point to the City Council, which was meeting inside. This was one of many such demonstrations in city after city that brought some much needed help to starving people.

On my own behalf, I asked for financial help from the school several times, but such help went mostly to those who were looked on as potential stars.

I continued to study at Curtis until the spring of 1939, and although my tuition was free, I had to work for my living. For several years, I went back to Seattle for the November to February symphony season.

What I could save from the Seattle Symphony salary, which increased to twenty-five and then to thirty-five dollars a week, paid my food and lodging in Philadelphia with the help of a few dollars a week from Franz. Later I was able to remain throughout the school year, picking up a few musical jobs, and playing in a WPA orchestra.

After a summer trip to Mexico where I got amoebic dysentery, I returned to school thin and wan. I planned to ask for financial help once more and just to assure that I looked properly needy, I stayed up all night before going in to the office.

I was greeted with a horrified, "Russell!" and for that term got my lunches paid for by the school.

I was not the only student suffering from the depression. When I was living on the second floor of a rooming house, another Curtis student was in a room just below me. His father was quite unable to help his son, as he was a junk man in another city who made a scanty living picking up old iron and selling it. At night, I could hear my friend's frantic prayers. He was literally starving.

At my insistence, we went to the school office and asked for—demanded—help for him. He got it. If he had been forced to give up school, the music world would have lost a fine musician. He became the principal of his section in one of the great orchestras.

Another student who was quite an influence was Fred Batchelder, with whom I maintained an alliance until his death. We lived together, played music together and cooked together during the last year and a half that I was at Curtis. Soon after I left, he married Jane Tyre, another fine bass player at Curtis. They later lived with us briefly in Los Angeles. Fred was a hard-driving bass player

Fred Batchelder and Russell applying themselves to their bass studies at Curtis

who was devoted to the profession and to the betterment of conditions for musicians. He also had a biting sense of humor, was remarkably courageous and an unyielding advocate for peace. Once during a demonstration against militarism, he went out in a canoe in New York harbor by himself and disrupted the path of the war ships on parade.

It was a difficult period, yet it was exciting, too. Side by side with the hunger and despair around me there was a growing determination for change. People were on the move, organizing for relief, for unemployment insurance, for work. Roosevelt was swept into office to do something about the terrible effects of the depression. (He didn't get my vote the first time around: too damned rich!) Within a few months, workers—for the first time in our history—had a legal right to unionize. They seized that right and went on the move in a big way.[4]

As some of these struggles bore fruit, people felt empowered. The more they sensed the potential in organized action, the more the movement grew. Like many other cultural workers, I was inspired by it and became a part of it. Although the school itself remained aloof and there were few non-musical student activities, it was impossible simply to study, unaffected by the world around us.

The years at Curtis were an exciting period for me musically. I was in contact with many fine musicians, both students and faculty. My horizons expanded, my skill and confidence increased, and I related music to the whole society in which I lived.

Early in my Philadelphia days I joined a friend's current events discussion group. Hilterism was on the rise, which we discussed as a serious threat. At the same time, nine southern African-American youth were accused of rape and threatened with both legal and actual lynching. The Scottsboro Boys case continued for years, growing into a worldwide struggle. I recall that I was fearful that our whole country could be torn to shreds. Ever since, I've understood that the fight against racism was central to bringing about peace, democracy, and justice.

In the Thirties, most of the leading musicians, including many of our teachers, were European-born and educated. Curtis was one of a few conservatories beginning to develop a new generation of U.S.-trained musicians.

The Curtis Institute of Music got its name and its endowment from the Curtis Publishing Co. Mary Louise Curtis Bok loved music and deserves to be honored for using her wealth in such a socially worthwhile and lasting way.

Curtis students, however, felt no particular loyalty to the publications whose circulation had produced the wealth that supported the school. This was amusingly demonstrated one day when about fifty of us were gathered in the student lounge waiting for one of our infrequent assemblies to take place. A small boy with a canvas bag of magazines came in and walked all around the room, offering the *Saturday Evening Post* and the *Ladies Home Journal* to each student without making a single sale.

Curtis had a student body of about 125. Students were of various ages. They did not go through a standard course and then graduate but studied until they were ready for professional work. One of the Institute's most famous alumni, Leonard Bernstein, entered after graduating from Harvard, while the youngest ever accepted, Sol Kaplan, had begun his Curtis piano lessons at age five in 1924. When I was there, Sol was still studying piano and composition. We became friends in spite of the difference in our ages. I enjoyed listening to him practice. He could play from memory almost any classical composition that I could name. Sol later chose composition as his life work. He may be best known for his work in the making of that wonderful, prize-winning film, *Salt of the Earth.*

We had some classes with other music students, for example in solfege and harmony, and many of us played in the school's orchestra or a chamber group, but most of our training was in a class with others playing the same instrument, or one-on-one with our teacher.

Anton Torello, my teacher, was principal in the bass section of the Philadelphia Orchestra and a master bass player. He was not particularly good at instructing or explaining, but superb at doing. I

Anton Torello, master bassist, Russell's teacher at Curtis

learned best when he took the instrument away from me and showed me how to play.

Torello had an important effect on symphonic bass playing. He knew how to develop a rich sound, emphasized the use of instruments capable of such sound, and taught many of the bass players who later led the sections of major orchestras. He was also an influence in the adoption of the French bow, which is held differently from the German bow. Although some bass-ists still use the latter, the French bow came into much more general use. Working with the Philadel-phia instrument maker, De Luccia, Torello developed a new design for bass bows.

Russell practicing

Curtis is at Rittenhouse Square, near the Academy of Music, the home of the Philadelphia Orchestra, then, as now, one of the country's greatest. Many of the Curtis teachers were members. Leopold Stokowski was in the midst of his many years as its conductor. He was an inspiring and innovative conductor, re-vered by many Philadelphians as almost a god of music.

Stokowski maintained that modern orchestral instruments not available in the days of Bach and other early composers made it possible to enrich the interpretation of their works with expanded instrumentation. I found the Stokowski interpreta-tion of these works thrilling. In Philadelphia Orchestra con-certs I also heard for the first time Shostakovitch's *Fifth Sym-phony* and Stravinsky's *Firebird*.

The school provided us with tickets for some concerts. In other cases, we stood in line to get the cheapest seats, some-times getting rained on or dripped on by the pigeons.

We students had the opportunity to hear a great deal of music on a level far higher than anything I had previously experi-enced. It was an inspiring atmosphere for the study of music.

Recordings now make the music of the great orchestras ac-cessible to music students no matter how remote they may be from the big centers of music, but what I had heard on our wind-up phonograph or in the concerts of the little Seattle Sym-phony had only hinted at what orchestra music could be.

Within the school, too, there were musical experiences that enlarged my understanding and expanded my interests. Bela Bartok, the great Hungarian composer, came to Curtis to perform his piano pieces for children. He opened the door for me not only to his music but also to a gradually increasing appreciation of many modern composers, such as Hindemith and Kodaly, who made the once-scorned Debussy seem tame.

After my first year, I played in the Curtis Orchestra. Several years later, when Torello felt I had become sufficiently accomplished, he promoted me to principal of the bass section.

A thrilling experience was participating in the first rehearsal of a new work, *Adagio for Strings* by Samuel Barber, a talented recent graduate of Curtis. It was in manuscript and was, I believe, being run through for the first time. Since then, it has entranced millions of listeners.

To me as a student, Fritz Reiner was a giant of a conductor and musician. To play under him in the Curtis Orchestra was a great learning experience.

When Bela Bartok was suffering from cancer and dying in poverty, it was Reiner who arranged to get financial and medical help for his fellow countryman. If, along with the three Bs—Bach, Beethoven and Brahms—there were to be a fourth, I would nominate Bartok. Thank you, Fritz; helping him was an act of real decency.

But Reiner had another side. Hershey Kaye was an outstanding student, one of the most talented. He applied to Reiner to join his conducting class. The master put Hershey through a stiff test and interrogation. After each successful answer, Fritz seemed to become more angry. Finally, he dismissed Hershey, not on the grounds of his musicianship but because he was "too short." Actually, Reiner himself was little taller. Kaye was an exceptional young musician, and he was always upbeat. His family was among the most generous of my experience. His father was in the printing business and provided anti-fascist organizations with almost unlimited paper for printing leaflets and other material. Hersh, as far as I know, never became a conductor but was a top-notch arranger and orchestrator. He died too young.

Even worse was a painful incident in the Curtis Orchestra under Reiner. A new young student bass player (also short) came into the orchestra rehearsal on a trial basis. In the middle of the *Meistersinger Overture*, Reiner stopped the orchestra, glared at the kid, pointed his finger at him and shouted, "You! Get out!"

The kid put down his bass and left. We never saw him again. I didn't sleep that night. At that point I vowed never to let such an incident pass without at least registering my disapproval. This was not a simple matter because at that time the conductor in any orchestra was an unquestioned autocrat. Nevertheless, I believed that while a conductor's talent should be appreciated and his musical direction followed, his domineering should be resisted. The idea that an orchestra is a conductor's instrument turns people into things, mere strings and keys to be played upon.

During my seasons in the Seattle Symphony, I was fortunate that Basil Cameron had replaced Karl Kruger as conductor. Cameron gave me a kind of help most unusual for a conductor. He coached me once a week.

Whether he felt that I needed improvement more than anyone else in the orchestra, or whether he singled me out because he saw me as particularly young and talented, I never knew. Whatever it was, he helped me on the way to becoming a good symphony musician.

Yet he, too, was sometimes insensitive and rude to the musicians. Whenever the first cellist had a solo, he would get a sour look from Cameron. If the cellist was having difficulty with the passage, this made it all the harder for him to play well.

"Give the bastard the same kind of look right back," I advised him, but he couldn't break the habit established by years of accepting whatever the conductor handed out.

Later, Cameron yelled at me for some reason. I yelled right back and never got yelled at again. The cellist was amazed. He must have wondered why he, a well-established first chair man, couldn't oppose the conductor while a young section player could do so.

I think it had something to do with that experience with Reiner. Perhaps it also came from my life with my authoritarian father, which had given me distaste for authoritarianism in any setting. Then too, I was gaining respect, not just for myself as an individual, but for the profession of which I was becoming a part. I felt that *all* its practitioners deserved respect.

Torello, like many of the Curtis teachers who were accomplished musicians, was almost idolized by many of his students, but it was no longer in me to be worshipful.

One cold winter day Torello came late to the bass class and found me sitting in his chair, reading the newspaper. I got up, of course, and when he was sitting down, he remarked, "Mm, Seattle heat."

Then he noticed that I had been reading the front page.

"You're reading the wrong section," he said. "You should be reading this," and he turned the paper over to the comic strips.

"I guess you read this," I responded, turning to the financial page. (It was rumored that he had lost heavily on the stock exchange.) He acknowledged as much by groaning and hitting his forehead with the heel of his hand.

I turned back to the front page. "Perhaps you should have been reading this!"

It was a blow to me when I was replaced as principal of the bass section by another student who, though versatile, seemed to me no better a bassist than I. He had made a point of meeting Torello at the door, taking his coat, carrying his music, and generally giving him the "maestro" treatment.

I was upset. Jane Tyre, one of the other bass students, sympathized. We went for a long walk through the snow up the Wissahickon, which settled me down.

Torello was a Spanish royalist and a personal friend of King Alfonso, the deposed king of Spain. When General Francisco Franco and the other insurgent generals attacked the democratically elected government of the new Spanish Republic in 1936, Torello's friendship with Alfonso led him to sympathize with the insurgents in spite of their alliance with Nazi Germany and Fascist Italy.

My sympathies were all the other way. I helped to organize one concert to raise money for North American Aid for Spanish Democracy and played in another.

Torello invited me to dinner at his house, the only time he had ever done so, and tried to convince me that in performing for Republican Spain, I was supporting the wrong side.

The concert for Spain was one of many at the Music Center, part of the flourishing left cultural movement in the city, which included performing groups like the Theater Arts Committee and writing and graphic arts groups as well.

The Music Center was organized by progressive musicians with Communist leadership to give low cost instruction to students who could not afford to study elsewhere and to organize musical performances for progressive causes. I became part of it during my second year at Curtis and continued throughout the Thirties, teaching bass and performing in chamber groups.

The Music Center brought my musical and my growing social/political interests together. The concert for Republican Spain, for example, gave me an opportunity to contribute in a small way to the struggle against fascism and to do so by playing Schubert's *Trout Quintet* together with some accomplished students who later went on to careers in major orchestras or in Hollywood: Eudice Shapiro, violinist; Phil Goldberg, violist; Victor Gottlieb, cellist; Sol Kaplan, pianist. I liked and admired several of my Center associates who were Jewish, which brings me to another important influence in my student years. I had never known Jews in Spokane or Seattle. Now many of my fellow students were Jews. Curtis was one of the all-too-few institutions of higher learning that did not impose a quota on Jewish admissions.

Also, not only at school and in the Music Center, but in other progressive activities, I frequently met Jews. Most intimate was the experience of living with Jewish families who surrounded me with warm friendship and opened a door for me to a different and fascinating culture.

It began in a little delicatessen on Germantown Avenue where Franz and I stopped to buy food when we were in the city for my Curtis audition. Old Mr. and Mrs. Shechter, who waited on us, were so helpful and friendly that when I returned for the school term, I went back to the store to ask if they could help me find a cheap place to live.

Their son and daughter-in-law took me in and charged me very little. Their parents had fled persecution in Czarist Russia, so they had grown up in this country. Nevertheless, they were still steeped in the folklore of the shtetl. However, they lived a long, long walk from the school, and I couldn't afford the subway fare. I often broke the journey at the Rodin Museum on the parkway, where I never tired of looking at the sculptures, or at the Public Library, where I browsed among the art books.

The following year I looked for a place a little closer, and was directed by the school to another Jewish family, the Gechtoffs, who were also more than kind to me and continued my Jewish education.

As I became more active in the progressive movement in later years, still another Jewish family, the Martins, took me in. I lived with them in the Carl Mackley Apartments, one of the first low-cost housing developments of the New Deal era. George Martin was an organizer for the shoe workers union, and Sylvia worked in the office of another union. They had two small boys.

By the time I left Philadelphia, I had added a number of colorful Yiddish sayings to my vocabulary and claimed to be a Jew by osmosis.

Learning of the long history of persecution Jews had endured, I admired their steadfastness and their resistance. This added to the growth of my anti-fascism.

While some people looked on the Nazis as mere crackpots, others sensed the danger in the rise of fascism, saw signs of it even in our own country, and feared this madness might envelop the world.

Some of us at Curtis felt we must do what we could to struggle against it, as in our concerts for Spain. At the same time, we were engaged in an intense effort to excel in our profession. It was difficult to strike a balance between these two imperatives. We performed for anti-fascist causes, raised money, and joined demonstrations. Our small efforts were inspirational to other Philadelphia youth.

Especially in my first years, simply living was a problem. My Jewish friends helped with cheap housing, but I still had to eat. I usually had a hot plate on which to warm up canned soup. My diet was otherwise heavy on oatmeal mush, bread and peanut butter, apples and fig bars.

There were weekly teas at Curtis, which I welcomed because I was always hungry and could fill up on cookies. These teas had another purpose, however, which was less welcome. Besides wanting us to become fine musicians, the Curtis administration wanted us to learn how to behave like ladies and gentlemen. That did not come naturally to me. At one of the teas, a pickle dropped on the floor. I picked it up so no one would slip on it.

Miss Hoopes from the office reproved me. "No, no. That's for the help to do."

A few days later, four of us students were walking by the office, and while two stopped in with a question for her, one other and I waited just outside the door.

I called out, "Hurry up, you lugs, you're keeping two gentle-men waiting." Even Miss Hoopes couldn't help laughing.

The economy improved in 1935 and 1936. For instance, I played in the Seattle Symphony at the San Diego World's Fair in the summer of 1935 for the munificent salary of $70 a week. However, in 1937, there was another slump.

Nevertheless, I was able to remain at Curtis throughout the school term from mid-September to May. This was possible in part because of the struggles of the unemployed for work or relief and the establishment of the Works Progress Administra-tion (WPA). I first had to go on relief, which I could now do, and then get on WPA. I joined the WPA Symphony, which played free concerts for schools and for institutions such as the one named, in wrought iron over the entrance gate, "Home of the Incurables." How brutal can you get?

There were some very fine musicians in that orchestra. I particularly remember the concertmaster, a short, jolly, roly-poly fellow who played the hell out of his fiddle.

The WPA arts program kept many performing artists, graphic artists, and writers alive during those depression years. The work they did contributed to one of the most vital artistic peri-ods in our history. The orchestra in which I played brought music to many people who otherwise would never have heard it. Of even more significance were compositions, paintings, murals, plays and books that would never have been possible without that government support.

Much of this work had social meaning and this horrified some members of Congress, who regarded government support of the arts as socialistic, no matter what its meaning. Art with a message was downright evil. There had to be constant efforts to press for continuation of the program. It was repeatedly trimmed and finally destroyed.

We were paid the standard WPA weekly salary, about $21 a week. Someone in Washington learned that we were not put-ting in full workdays like other WPA workers. From then on we were required to be in the rehearsal hall eight hours a day whether or not we were playing. Rehearsing and concertizing requires intense concentration. It is impossible to rehearse for eight consecutive hours, so we whiled away the time playing cards. Of course, this schedule made it difficult to keep up with my musical studies.

How I managed escapes me now. I probably had to cut down on class work and schedule my lessons after WPA hours.

The school administration considered it a scandal for a Curtis student, an embryo artist, to be on relief. But as the recession continued, more and more students were without money and even without food. The school could not come to the rescue of all who needed help. Curtis administrators must have decided that scandal was preferable to starvation and sent several students to me so I could help them get on relief.

I continued at Curtis for the full term in 1938-39. I was able to get off WPA and get a few music jobs, including—best of all— a short season with the Philadelphia Opera.

I picked up a few dance jobs, although I was not in a regular band. A contractor would put together a group for a particular job. This made it difficult to respond collectively to a boss who treated us unfairly.

On one out-of-town job, we had been promised good transportation and adequate pay. The contractor made a mess of everything. We had a lousy bus to carry us from Philadelphia to Pittsfield. We set up in the wrong fraternity house and had to carry our instruments about a block in the rain, and so on. When we got on the bus to return to Philadelphia, he announced a cut in our pay. Then he sat down beside me, probably choosing to do so because I looked like a nice clean-cut American boy, easier to deal with than the older and presumably more militant Jews and Italians who made up the rest of the group. I didn't appreciate the honor. He got hell from me for the duration of the trip.

I well knew, however, that individual talk was not enough. This was one of the experiences that helped to make an organized activist of me. My family background predisposed me to progressive politics, but it took a spark from my own experience to propel me forward, to teach me that just to be angry at what is wrong is meaningless. Controlled and organized anger can become productive.

In 1937, I shared housing with a professional musician and his wife. He was a graduate of Curtis I had met through the Music Center and was a Communist. In that year, I too became a Communist.

At first I belonged to the Communist Musicians Club. Then one day, three of us Curtis students were talking politics. One was a leader in the Young Communist League. The other was younger and had not joined any organization but came from a Communist family. We were all deeply concerned about the rising fascism in Germany, its smashing of democracy, its persecution of Jews, Communists, trade unionists. With the country again in recession, it seemed that the capitalist system was incapable of feeding and housing its people and providing them with jobs. All three of us were committed to anti-fascism in the present and socialism in the future.

We decided to organize a Communist Club among Curtis students. We found a couple of others willing to join us. Together we educated ourselves through our own study and with the help of invited speakers on the principles of Marxism, and on current problems in our own country and the world. We also tried to reach other Curtis students with these ideas, to draw them into performing for progressive causes and sometimes invited them to join our group, which grew from the initial nucleus of three to eight or nine.

The Party leadership considered it important that we not jeopardize our education or our careers in music, so we could not be active publicly as Communists. However, we were publicly active anti-fascists, and were, of course, suspected by some of being Communists, a label that, deserved or not, was—and still is—often applied to any militant progressive.

One of our members was warned by her piano teacher that she should not associate with "that crowd." She ignored his instructions.

We were once having a meeting in an upstairs apartment over a store. Up the steps came a fellow student who was definitely not one of us. Our host went to the head of the stairs and politely asked him to come at another time. Although he left, he subsequently complained to the academic teacher about our having a "secret meeting." Her response was, "Possibly they have a community of interests."

We scattered after leaving Curtis, and I lost contact with most of my Curtis comrades and the other students who had worked with us on one issue or another. I do know that several made major contributions to society, musically and politically, some in major symphony orchestras, others elsewhere.

I was sadly reminded of one of them when the Curtis newsletter came with word of Sol Kaplan's death at age 71 on November 14, 1990. From early on, I felt honored to have Sol

Kaplan's friendship. Some of the films for which he wrote music were listed, merely scratching the surface of his life's work in music. His compositions were not all for films, but in that medium he should be remembered for one that was not mentioned: the score of *Salt of the Earth.*

He was one of that splendid group of artists who, after being blacklisted in Hollywood during the McCarthy period, produced one of the best films ever made in this country. Their independent company challenged the cultural, political, and economic dominance of the big movie corporations and the Cold War government restrictions on freedom of expression. *Salt of the Earth* is one of the few films ever made about the men and—with a rare understanding—the women of the working class. It is as meaningful today as it was when it was made in the Fifties. Its humanity and its artistry showed up the shallowness and falseness of the typical Hollywood product.

Hollywood and the FBI succeeded in keeping the film off the nation's screens and making it impossible for the company to produce more pictures. Yet *Salt of the Earth* received international acclaim and has become a lasting part of the culture of our country, and of international working class culture as well.[5]

My last few student years were very busy. Study, work, and political activity filled my days. The shadow of coming war was deepening. We saw our own country abandon the democratic government of Spain to the fascists, Britain appease Hitler at Munich, and the capitalist countries repeatedly refuse to join the Soviet Union in collective security.

When the war began in 1939, we had no confidence that it would be an anti-fascist war. When Torello offered to recommend me for a position in one of the military bands that was looking for a bass player, I had no hesitation in refusing. He was angry at my refusal.

My student years probably extended longer than necessary, although my studies had been constantly interrupted by my need to work. My problem was that I tended to undervalue my own musicianship and was slow to develop confidence in my readiness for a career in a major symphony. I was so nervous if I had to play an audition that I did not seek them out, although I was well equipped by training and experience to apply for a post in the bass section of any of the country's symphonies.

This seems in contradiction to my willingness to stand up to conductors and to be active and outspoken in my political life.

In retrospect, I think my feeling of inadequacy may have come in part from what seemed to be the little value I had in my father's eyes when I was a child. With five older siblings, I felt not only younger but also lesser than they. It took me many years and much encouragement to overcome those feelings.

One such encouraging episode occurred near the end of my student years. I was rehearsing in the school auditorium with a small group in which I was the only bass. The doors were open, which made it possible for anyone entering the building to hear the music but not to see the musicians. As one of my friends later told me, Torello came in, listened for a few minutes and without knowing that I was the performer said, "That's the way I want my bass players to sound!"

At the end of the 1938-39 school year, I left Curtis, headed for a visit to the family and a vacation in Seattle. By the fall I expected to be in Los Angeles where there was a symphony as well as many music jobs in the film industry.

MOUNTAINS AND MARRIAGE

When I left Philadelphia, I knew I would never go back. Many Curtis students aspired to membership in the Philadelphia Orchestra, but that was not for me. I was reconciled to the fact that I could ply my trade only in a city large enough to have a symphony orchestra, but not in a big, dirty, crowded eastern city if I could help it. I hoped to find a place in Los Angeles or another western city.

First, I was eager to vacation among the mountains and waters of the Pacific Northwest that I had missed so much.

My family had gone through many changes. My younger brother, Spencer, was no longer with us. He had joined the orchestra on a ship sailing to Alaska even though he was not feeling well. He developed acute appendicitis, the medical care on board was inadequate, and he died.

All three of my sisters were married, and I attended Franz's wedding in Michigan on my way home. Cecelia had made painting, not music, her major interest, but Franz and Sigrid continued to play fiddle, Juliet cello, and Voltaire piano, harp and accordion. All of them did some performing and some teaching. Although I was the only one in the family to make a lifelong career of music, it has always been an important part of the lives of my brothers and sisters.

They also continued to take an interest in issues of peace and justice. Cecelia and Juliet, in particular, have been active in the peace movement.

In Seattle, I stayed with my mother, who now lived alone in an apartment Franz had built for her with my help during a previous vacation. With her many children grown and gone, it was adequate for her, and she could rent out the main part of the house.

I spent much of my time with my brothers and sisters. I had been back only a week or two when Voltaire and I set out on a five-week canoe trip.

We put our canoe in the water at Golden Gardens, crossed Elliott Bay, and spent our days along Puget Sound and Hood

Canal, sometimes paddling, sometimes putting our sail up to let the wind do the work. At night we camped on shore, often feasting on oysters, berries and other fruit that were ours for the picking. From time to time we replenished our supplies in one of the small shore towns.

The Olympic Mountains were to the west of us, the Cascades more distantly to the east. Heavily wooded hills rose steeply from the water in some places; elsewhere there were scattered farms and summer cottages. We never had trouble finding a place on the beach to make a fire and roll out our bedding.

Most of the days were beautiful, and if we had a little rain from time to time, that was only to be expected in a Northwest summer. The water was cold, but not too cold for an occasional swim. The nights were cold, too, but we had plenty of blankets and contrived a shelter when rain threatened with a big canvas and the canoe turned upside down.

Voltaire had spent much more time in the canoe than I had. He was daring about taking the canoe out into high winds and rough water. That made for some exciting times. We always came through until one day near the end of our trip.

Voltaire with canoe

We had the sail up. A gust of wind caught us unaware. The canoe tipped, dumping us in the water and sending our equipment floating out of our reach or sinking to the bottom. We made it to shore and sighted the canoe floating off on its side with the sail dragging in the water. We ran along the beach in pursuit.

It would have been difficult enough if this had been a sandy beach, but it was rough and rocky, with many barnacles clinging to the rocks. We couldn't stop to pick our way through. We had to overtake the current that was carrying the canoe along parallel to the beach. We finally caught up and plunged into the salt water, which stung our barnacle-scratched feet and legs. We waded and swam out and managed to drag the canoe, half full of water, to shore.

Russell with canoe

Probably because the canoe had not turned completely upside down, the paddles were still there—the only pieces of equipment that survived, but the most essential ones. Without them, the old saying about being "up the creek without a paddle" would have been all too true.

We lost no time in heading for home. It was too cold that night to sleep, so we paddled all night and by morning made it to Elliott Bay, then up through the locks to Lake Union and finally to safe haven near the Montlake Bridge.

Cecelia and her husband, Bill Corr, lived not far way, on Roosevelt Way, so we made for their home by alleys and back ways. Each of us was barefoot, badly in need of a shave and a haircut, with no clothes but well-worn and salt-water-soaked swimming trunks.

As I walked through the back door into Cecelia's kitchen, the first person I saw was a total stranger. Virginia Warner was a friend of Cecelia and Bill who was living with them to help out while Cecelia was pregnant with her second child. Virginia was peacefully ironing the clothes when we appeared in all our glory. She recognized Voltaire, so she wasn't completely taken aback, but it certainly can't be said that I walked into her life in an aura of romance.

Virginia was working half-days in the office of the Washington Old Age Pension Union. This was a progressive senior organization fighting for decent state pensions and for federal social security. When she came home that evening, her second view of me was, if anything, even less romantic. True, I was now clean and shaved, but I was hunched over a bucket of water, with my pants rolled up, soaking my sore feet.

A week or so later, I came over to spend the evening with Cecelia since both Bill and Virginia had meetings. I mentioned that I had a couple of letters to write, so Virginia told me to feel free to use her desk. She was a writer, and in between working at the Pension Union and organizing domestic workers, she was researching the women's rights movement of the nineteenth century. Standing in a row at the back of her desk were *The History of Woman Suffrage, The Biography of Susan B. Anthony, A Vindication of the Rights of Women* by Mary Wollstonecraft, August Bebel's *Women and Socialism* and *Lenin on the Woman Question.*

When Virginia came home, I was sitting at her desk. I looked at her, looked at the books, looked back at her and shook my head. "I sure feel sorry for some guy," I said.

Contrary to what one might expect, that was not the end of it. It was more like the beginning. She laughed at my jibe, recognizing that I was not really a sexist. Sharing humor has been an enduring part of our life together. I really admired her serious work on women's struggle for equality, and in our years together we always appreciated and supported each other's professional and political work.

Had I stuck to my original intention to leave Seattle for Los Angeles at the end of the canoeing vacation, both of our lives would have been different. However, I was offered the first chair in the bass section of the Seattle Symphony and decided to stay. A season as principal would be an important addition to my record.

Virginia and I spent many hours with Bill and Cecelia. The four of us made a regular thing of producing a special dinner on Saturday and spending the evening in talk. With a nod to Bobby Burns, we called those occasions "The Cotters' Saturday Night." Bill was a great storyteller with a sharp wit. He was also a serious student of Marxism with a lot of political experience behind him. One could not participate in a discussion with him without learning, not because of what he told us, but because he challenged us to think.

Virginia and I also had time alone together, including a brief trip into the Cascades where we camped beside a mountain stream. By the middle of the Symphony season, we were lovers.

When the season was over, I was reluctant to leave Virginia. My acknowledged reason for staying in Seattle was that when I got to Los Angeles, union rules would not allow me to take music jobs for six months, so I needed some other way to earn a living in the meantime. I enrolled in a National Youth Administration training course for welders.

Russell and Virginia courting in Roslyn, Washington

Welding was much in demand in the booming war industry. It looked more and more likely that the United States would get into the war. At that point, I was still unconvinced that we should do so. Welding would give me some security while I was getting established in music and if war came, might keep me out of the actual fighting.

The closer my departure for California came, the less were Virginia and I ready to part. We married in October 1941. Our wedding was almost as unconventional as our first meeting.

Virginia's Republican Baptist father and stepmother were visiting from Denver, which meant that we must be married by a minister. This was something of a problem, but it was solved by the Reverend Pettus, known throughout the progressive movement as "Dad." Virginia's Aunt Rene, who had been close to her, especially since her mother's death, wanted Virginia to marry but was never satisfied with any of her boyfriends, including me. We asked her if we could be married in her apartment, which focused her attention on the preparations instead of on my qualifications.

Dad Pettus asked us if we wanted a long or a short ceremony. We chose the latter. It proved to be so short as to be almost sudden. Aunt Rene then hosted a supper for our small but very mixed group of guests ranging from Republican through progressive to Communist. Dad Pettus tried to recruit Aunt Rene into the Pension Union, which she regarded as insulting, since she was not yet of retirement age. Fortunately, Bill and Cecelia had brought their three-year-old son along. Johnny was a charming attention-getter on a totally apolitical level.

Virginia and I then climbed into my 1934 Chevrolet. I set off with a flourish, made a wide U-turn, hit the curb, and got a flat tire. So our married life began with me fixing a tire while Virginia sat on the curb.

A couple of weeks later, we piled my bass trunk and her typewriter and books into a trailer, hitched it behind the Chevy, tied a piece of red cloth on the protruding end of the bass trunk and set

Virginia with the bass trunk on the road from Seattle to Los Angeles

off down the coast. That red "flag" was a warning to other cars on the road, but to us it was also a symbol of our political convictions.

To the end of Virginia's life, fifty-eight years later, we journeyed together, still in agreement that teaming up was one of the best things we ever did, and still committed to socialism.

WAR YEARS IN LOS ANGELES

While I was enjoying my stay in the Northwest, Hitler attacked the Soviet Union. A week after our arrival in Los Angeles, Japan attacked Pearl Harbor. Like millions of other people in the country and the world, our personal lives were overshadowed for the next five years by the war.

Like my parents, I could never accept the slogan, "My country, right or wrong," but in this war I believed our country was basically on the right side. It was a war that could have been avoided had the Spanish Republicans not been abandoned to Franco and his Italian and German fascist supporters; had Hitler not been appeased at Munich; had the line been drawn against the Nazi advance into Czechoslovakia.

But now the war was a fact. With the world's first socialist country and my own country under attack, I had no choice but to support it. Yet I have opposed every war in which our country has been involved since, and there have been all too many, usually not called war until they are over. The names of the deadly games have been getting more imaginative: We have had a "police action" in Korea, the "defense of South Vietnam against Communist aggression," an "incursion" into Cambodia, an "Operation Just Cause" in Panama, and a "Desert Storm" in Iraq. All should have been spelled w-a-r.

In 1941, married men my age were not being drafted, but now I wanted to get into the war effort rather than out of it. I looked at welding in a very different way, gave up the idea of music and went to work for Calship, thinking it was probably for the duration of the war. There I was helping to build "Liberty ships" to carry war materiel and personnel to the fronts.

The workdays began very early because they were extended by the thirty-mile drive between Los Angeles and the shipyard in Wilmington. It took me a while to adjust to the early morning departure for work. One morning I overslept.

I jumped out of bed, threw on my clothes, grabbed my lunch box (packed the night before) and took off down the street in my car to pick up the co-worker with whom I shared rides.

I had not gone many blocks when a cop pulled me over. "You're exceeding the speed limit, you ran a red light, and you have an out-of-state plate. Let me see your license."

I reached for my wallet, only to find that in my haste, I had left it at home.

"Where are you going?"

"To work in the shipyards."

A slight pause and then he said, "Oh . . . zip up your fly and go to work."

It was hard, miserable work. Our schedule was designed to keep the work going twenty-four hours a day, seven days a week. I was fortunate in being on day shift, but never had a weekend off. It was five days of work and one day off, and every six weeks a thirteen-day stretch without a day off.

At least I got a regular paycheck. My weekly take-home pay was about fifty-two dollars. It enabled us to live in a style to which neither of us had been accustomed in the depression years. My pay for the year was just over three thousand dollars, far below today's poverty line, but at 1940 prices, almost adequate. We could bring home two big bags of groceries and meat for five dollars.

Together with Phil Goldberg, a violist and friend from Curtis days, we rented a house on Crenshaw Boulevard from a woman who must have been destined to be a landlady from birth—her name was Clementine Pratt. After about a year, she evicted us. Ostensibly it was because we didn't take good care of the yard. Probably it was because rent control was going into effect. She would not have been able to raise the rent on tenants in residence, but if she could get us out for cause, she could set the rent for the rest of the war at a higher level.

Phil's sister, Esther, lived with us for a while. She was a former nightclub dancer, now an assembly-line worker and shop steward in a shop making radio equipment for the army.

Esther had a boyfriend in the service who came to visit when he was on leave. He seemed surprised to find her consorting with a classical musician, but she assured him that though I was a "square," I was a "hep square." A high compliment.

Virginia went to work for the Los Angeles bureau of the *Daily People's World*, a west coast newspaper published in San Francisco. It had its beginnings in a Communist waterfront paper put out during the longshoremen's strike of the mid-thirties and was supported by many progressive unions.

Virginia's schedule was basically a standard five-day week, so we seldom had a day off together. She did the cooking and packed my lunches on my workdays. I often spent my day off cooking up a big stew, a roast or a spaghetti sauce to help us through the following week.

When I first started in the shipyard, all my fellow workers were white, many of them so-called "Okies" from Oklahoma or the other dust bowl states. Some had first come west to pick fruit in the Thirties, others more recently, attracted by jobs in war industry.

CIO unions had begun to break down the racial barriers in work and in unions in the Thirties, and now the war effort required every available worker. Washington required fair employment practices, and willingly or reluctantly, companies and old-line AFL unions with exclusionary rules began to comply.

When the rumors began to fly that "the Negroes are coming," some workers swore they would never work beside a Negro. Yet a few weeks later, more than one of those people was walking between the ways shoulder-to-shoulder with a black co-worker or eating lunch by his side. The transition was not smooth everywhere, but I did not observe any serious problems on my ship.

My only music jobs were a few concerts with the Janssen Orchestra for which rehearsals and concerts were scheduled in the evening or on Sundays.

Werner Janssen had conducting ambitions and money enough to hire an orchestra. It was made up mostly of musicians who played for the Hollywood studios and welcomed the chance to do some classical music.

One memorable musical experience occurred when the Communist Club to which I belonged planned a party to raise money for the *Daily People's World*. The paper was financially dependent on its readers, who raised money in an annual fund drive.

Our club was made up of shipyard workers who were in the Boilermakers Union. One had a home with a large living room where our party could be held. We planned to invite some of the people with whom we worked as well as advertising our event in the paper.

When we were planning the program, one of my comrades said, "Russ, you're a musician. Why don't you play for us?"

"The bass isn't a solo instrument," I objected.

When they persisted, I agreed to get a few musicians together to play some chamber music. Of course, what I had in mind was my favorite, Schubert's *Trout Quintet.*

I had no trouble finding a violinist, a violist, and a cellist. It was harder to locate a pianist who was both accomplished and willing to perform for the benefit of the *People's World.* Finally, someone steered me to a man who was the leading pianist at one of the studios. He was completely apolitical but passionately fond of chamber music, and he jumped at the chance to do the *Trout.*

When the night of the party came, I had more than the usual pre-performance nervousness. I felt responsible for its success, both to the musicians who had devoted evenings to rehearsing, and to my comrades who had trusted me to entertain our guests. There was no need to worry. We could not have played for a more attentive and appreciative audience.

Recounting the surface events in our personal lives cannot possibly convey the feeling of those years. We on the home front escaped the fighting and dying; nevertheless, the war was the reality that dominated our days. The news from the Pacific front and the European front preoccupied us.

Great questions were being decided in that fighting: Would the fascism that had been marching across Europe and had reached around the world to ally itself with Imperial Japan rule the world? Would socialism survive in the Soviet Union? Would China have a chance to free itself from Japanese dominance and overcome the dead hand of feudalism?

We felt confident of ultimate victory for the anti-fascist US-USSR-Britain-France-China alliance that should have been formed in the Thirties but was now a reality. We also felt sure that this would lead to a more democratic U.S. when the war was over.

Our concern now was everything to win the war, everything for war production, lend-lease to all allies, Russian War Relief, agitation for a second front in Europe. The Soviets were bearing the brunt of the fighting in Europe; an attack by the Allies across the English Channel was essential.

In our own country, the war sometimes seemed to have changed everything. Instead of unemployment lines, there were more jobs than there were people to do them. A few of the barriers to African-Americans in industry were breached. Women, instead of being told their place was at home, were told it was their patriotic duty to take a job—the very jobs they had always been told only men could and should do.

Instead of constantly protesting the injustices of capitalism and its government, we were now in the mainstream, supporting that government in its war effort.

The Soviet Union, which ever since 1917 had been pictured as the epitome of everything that was wrong and bad, was now being called our brave ally. On November 7, the anniversary of the Russian revolution, the Soviet flag with its hammer and sickle was raised to wave beside the Stars and Stripes over the Los Angeles City Hall.

Arbitration and a no-strike pledge by the unions replaced the battles between unions and corporations. Rent and price controls were supposed to protect the people's livelihood and did help considerably. However, the patriotic duty of business to put the nation's needs before their profits was honored more in the breach than in the observance.

We were swept into the feeling that we were all on the same side. We seemed to have no enemies at home except those whose anti-Soviet sentiment or profiteering obstructed the war effort. We even had hopes for the extension of the alliance with the Soviet Union after the war.

My shipyard work continued through most of the war years until I could no longer weld. In spite of goggles and helmet, my eyes were being affected. I quit my shipyard job and was, of course, called up by the Draft Board. However, because of my bad eyes, I was rated 4F, not acceptable for service for physical reasons.

Now it was back to music. First came a little work in the film studios. There were some more or less stable orchestras attached to particular studios, but much of the work was freelance. That meant seeing to it that contractors knew I was qualified and available. It meant being on call whenever I was wanted. The pay was good for that time, but it was feast or famine. I might go for weeks without a call, and then make two hundred dollars in one concentrated work session.

Our income dropped, but we were confident that the music work would pick up, confident enough to decide it was time to have a child. Virginia was soon pregnant, and we began house hunting.

As I have mentioned before, I am a cooperation buff, and so was Virginia. What one of us could not do alone we could sometimes do together. What the two of us could not do alone, we might be able to do in cooperation with others.

So we had done better during the wartime housing shortage by sharing our housing for the most part with one or more Goldbergs.

Now, although we had a little money saved for a down payment on a house, we thought we might do better together with friends, and proposed a joint house hunt with our friends Carl and Gerda Lerner. They liked the idea, but after a few ventures into the real estate market decided they were not ready to buy.

So we proceeded on our own and found what we thought would be our lifetime home in the Echo Park district. It was a two-story redwood shingle house with big redwood trees in front and back, ample for the family we planned to have.

We had been warned not to buy in those times of high wartime prices, and the $6,500 price tag looked forbiddingly high to us, but we took the plunge. Contrary to predictions, real estate prices, which had been low in pre-war depression years, rose even more after the war.

When not working, I began to fix the house up. Ever since my first effort at construction in grade school when I built a birdhouse, I have liked working in wood and doing carpentry.

In December of 1944, our daughter Cynthia was born. I was playing a dance job that evening. I would much rather have been near Virginia, but jobs had not been plentiful, and we needed the money. I called the hospital during intermission and got the news: "It's a girl!"

A few months later, we welcomed Virginia's sister, Kendall Frazier, and her eighteen-month old son,

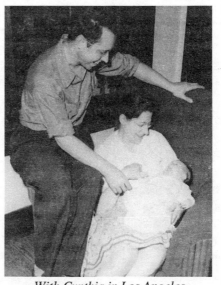

With Cynthia in Los Angeles

who came to live with us. Kendall's husband was in the Merchant Marine, shipping out from the East Coast. He was now about to change to Pacific ports, and she wanted to be where she could see him when he had shore leave.

Music work indeed picked up in 1945. I was added to the bass section of the Los Angeles Philharmonic for a special concert in April conducted by Arturo Toscanini. Shortly thereafter, I was hired for a summer season in the Hollywood Bowl under Leopold Stowkowski.

My first encounter with "Stoky" came before rehearsals started. He wanted to get a sense of the Bowl's acoustics. My bass had five strings, instead of the usual four, which meant that I could go a major third lower than most bass players. Stokowski had me on the stage playing low notes, and Jeanette McDonald singing high notes while he roamed around the Bowl, listening from different positions.

When rehearsals started, it was great to be playing under Stokowski some of the same compositions that had so impressed me when I was merely a listener, for example, Bach's *Toccata and Fugue in D Minor* that was almost his signature number.

This felt like the beginning of my peacetime life. The war in Europe had ended in May, and victory in the Pacific seemed certain to follow soon.

On the beach

It was great to get back to my bass fiddle and my bow instead of a welding machine, a long, snaky black lead, and a torch. Now I was doing what had always been—and I hoped always would be—part of my life.

In the Hollywood Bowl, there was a woman bassist on either side of me. Women were finding it less difficult to break into the symphonic field because of the wartime shortage of men. In every occupation it opened up a few new opportunities. Whether these would last after the war was uncertain. Suzanne Ailman, my stand partner, was trying to decide whether to continue in the profession and was being discouraged by her teacher, Kenneth Winstead, who was also playing in the section. Suzanne was certainly talented, and I thought she should keep trying.

My position was that if we truly loved music, we would not discourage half the talent. I sometimes taunted my sexist colleagues that they opposed women in the profession because they were afraid of the competition.

One amusing incident of the Bowl season occurred when Danny Kaye was the guest artist. Kaye liked music and musicians, was generous with his talents on behalf of pension benefit concerts, and was well liked in return. I once played a recording date with him when he insisted on perfection plus, simply in order to make sure that the musicians got in enough hours to make the date worthwhile.

In the Hollywood Bowl, while waiting to rehearse his own part, he stood behind the conductor and imitated his movements in a humorous way. We in the orchestra responded by a little clowning of our own. The contractor who had hired all of us for the job was sitting in the front row of the Bowl. He rose, obviously to reprove the musicians.

Before he could make so much as a gesture in that direction, Danny whirled, pointed a finger at him and said, "Sit down."

Taken aback, the contractor simply stood there.

"Sit down!" Kaye said again, more severely this time. Still no movement from the contractor.

For the third time, in a most authoritative manner, Kaye repeated, "SIT DOWN!"

The contractor sat down, to the intense pleasure of every orchestra member. Contractors were considered, for the most part, a necessary evil. They must be propitiated, but they were seldom liked.

I was a little premature in feeling at peace. The war was not yet over. Japan surrendered on September 2, but what happened in August far overshadowed the victory. On August 6, the U.S. dropped an atomic bomb on Hiroshima, and three days later another on Nagasaki.

These bombs, with their immense destruction of human life, were said to be justified as necessary to end the war. In retrospect, they seem more like the shots that began the Cold War.

At the time, we had no conception of what was to come. Close to home, however, we could see one of the first breaks in the peace between bosses and workers. This was the strike of the Conference of Studio Unions against the major film studios. It was a forerunner of the wave of militant strikes in the winter of 1945-46 in which the unions tried to catch up with the rising cost of living during the largest wave of strikes the country has ever seen.

The union situation in the film industry was complex. Film musicians belonged to the Los Angeles local of the AFM, along with members of the Symphony, nightclub performers, and others. They had no ties with the studio unions in the other various crafts, but that did not mean they were unaffected by the struggles of those other workers.

It was not unlike the situation in the mass production industries before the rise of the CIO, when skilled crafts were organized, each into its own union, with no contact with the main body of production workers.

Studio production workers were organized independently on a craft basis but were united in the Conference of Studio Unions (CSU).

Another union on the scene was the International Association of Theatrical and Stage Employees (IATSE). Corrupt and gangster-ridden, it sought an industry-wide lock on the various craft workers. Its method was not organizing for better pay and conditions, like the CSU, but by making an alliance with the studio heads and signing "sweetheart" agreements satisfactory to the bosses.

The CSU had a more democratic organization, more solid union policies, and more honest and progressive leadership than the IATSE. During the war, two long-time IATSE leaders went to jail and a new man, Roy Brewer, came to Hollywood, supposedly to clean up. It soon developed that while he was concerned with cleaning up the IATSE reputation for corruption, collusion with management would continue as before, or become even worse.

The effort of the Carpenter's Union, one of the affiliates of the CSU, to get a decent contract out of the studios was unsuccessful. The carpenters went on strike in March 1945, supported by the other unions in CSU.

We in the Communist Party were committed to the wartime no-strike pledge, and did not at first support this strike. Yet one of the main weapons being used against CSU was the claim that it was "Communist dominated." The studios made a deal with the IATSE and presented the strike as a jurisdictional dispute.

With the war approaching its end, Communist members of CSU urged a change in our position, and the Party began to support the long-drawn-out strike. My comrades in the Musician's Union and I were very much in agreement. We did not have to be affiliated with the CSU to know that if they lost the strike it would affect all of us who did studio work. The Musicians Union, however, officially supported the IATSE because both were AFL unions.

In October, there was an appeal by the CSU for a mass picket line in front of the Warner Brothers lot. I responded, along with many other progressive musicians and members of other unions.

Although my part in this dramatic event was very small, it was important to me. I believe that unity and solidarity are important principles, and practically speaking, the only way unions can maintain the strength to stand up to the power of the corporations. This appeal to join the picket line was a challenge to me to stand up for what I believed in spite of possible risk to myself. It was a situation in which I and others who depended on studio work at all would be putting our jobs on the line when we put our bodies on the line.

We had a big, spirited picket line in spite of scabs trying to break through and IATSE thugs attacking pickets by swinging lengths of heavy chain. When the Burbank police showed up, they ignored the violence of the IATSE thugs. Instead, they arrested the whole picket line and herded us onto the Warner Brothers lot. That was a scary moment.

It was scary particularly because it was illegal. The arrest of an entire line of peaceful pickets who were breaking no law was illegal, and the crime was compounded by making what was essentially a city jail out of the private property of a party to a

company vs. union dispute. It was a blatant abandonment of
the fiction that the government was an impartial dispenser of
justice. In a sudden reversal of the government-management-
union unity that had prevailed throughout the war, management was showing its teeth, and local government was obliging
by providing what were essentially company police.

Our feeling of collective strength, however, kept our spirits
up. Earl Robinson was there with his guitar and led us all in
singing labor songs. Earl Robinson had come into our acquaintance as a pianist on my second trip to Asia as a musician on
the President Line. During our performing duties, Earl would
sit at the keyboard and just doodle. We hardly had to play at all
until the passengers finished their meal. Another crew member, who needed cash at the end of the trip, sold Earl his first
guitar for $5. From that time on, we followed with interest Earl's
career as a singer and composer of such classics as "Joe Hill"
and "Ballad for Americans."

When Virginia got the news that the whole picket line had
been arrested and was waiting to find out what would happen,
she paced the floor with baby Cynthia who was teething. She
kept the baby quiet by singing, "Mummy, don't you scold me, if
I let out a wail/ Cause Daddy's in the Burbank jail."

About half a dozen of the strikers were charged. I don't remember exactly what the charges were. They had to appear in
court and got a slap on the wrist. The rest of us were finger-
printed, then released, and never charged.

Each of us musicians got a call from our union's studio representative, reproving us for our action. In response to my defense on behalf of democratic unionism, he sounded off on his
"forty years in the business." I ignored him.

The CSU strike was an early indicator of what happened
after the war. Workers' grievances, muted during the war on
behalf of national unity, broke out in a wave of militant strikes.
There were some important gains, but the anti-communism that
had also been muted when the Soviet Union was our ally was
revived in a virulent form as a weapon against all kinds of progressive organizations.

Although the 1945 CSU strike in which I participated was
won, the studio craft unions were later destroyed and militant
democratic unionism was undermined throughout the country
in what has been called "The Cold War Against Labor."[6]

A STORMY SEASON

Most important of the opportunities opening up for me in this period was a successful audition for the Los Angeles Philharmonic. I was to start with the opening of the 1945-46 season, replacing a serviceman who had formerly held the position but would not return.

The road to the first Philharmonic rehearsal proved to be a bumpy one. I was informed that the serviceman had returned. However, Charles White, the personnel manager, told me there was a possibility I could be added to the section as a ninth bass. Conductor Alfred Wallenstein liked my playing. He was out of town, but Charley would confer with him when he returned. So I still had hope.

Sure enough, Charley called me a few days later with the good news. I was to be an addition to the section. He gave me direct assurance that I was now a member of the Philharmonic and talked about arranging for the additional music required.

The bad news came a week later. A letter from Wilfrid Davis, Associate Manager of the Orchestra, announced that "it is necessary for us to exercise the clause in your contract pertaining to return of one of our former players who has been in service." My services "would not be required this year."

I immediately called Charley and got the explanation that the business office had made a mistake in counting the number of musicians who would be rehired, the budget had been allocated, and there was no money for a ninth bass. My response was that I had been hired. Davis's letter was irrelevant since I was not to replace the serviceman, but to be added. Charley had given me a verbal commitment to that effect and just because someone in the office couldn't count to ninety-one, that commitment was not wiped out. It had the force of a contract.

I called Spike Wallace, the union president. He tried to dissuade me from pressing my case, told me I should have gotten it in writing, even hung up on me when I persisted. I promptly called him back and asked when the next Board meeting would take place.

"All right, Russell, you'll go to work."

Spike called a day or two later and offered me a job in the Kansas City Orchestra, which was looking for a bass player.

I turned that down and submitted the case to the union board. Charley admitted the verbal agreement. The union sent me a letter stating that "the Board holds that you are definitely engaged." Copies went to the management and the conductor.

So after having been in and out, and again in and again out, I was now in. At last I was a member of a major symphony.

Wallenstein was a competent, though not inspiring conductor. When he was dissatisfied, he had a habit of slamming his baton down on the stand and groaning, "Jesus Christ."

Virginia sometimes took one look at me when I came home and asked, "What's the matter? Another 'Jesus Christ' rehearsal?" Nevertheless, I was glad to be making music again, glad to be where I seemed to belong. I was now in the Musicians' Club of the Party. I got more active in the union and took an interest in the future of the orchestra.

There was an opportunity to play under some fine guest conductors, notably Otto Klemperer whom I very much admired.

Cynthia in St. Louis

In one special Russian War Relief concert, he shared the podium with Igor Stravinsky. Each conducted half and met on the stage at mid-concert, which presented an amusing picture. Stravinsky was small and agile, Klemperer very large and almost ungainly. Even standing on the podium, Stravinsky had to reach up to shake Klemperer's hand—grasshopper and elephant.

Our Communist Club, with the help of other progressive musicians, started what we called a "Union Activities Committee." Its purpose was to encourage greater participation by the members and to move the union into more militant action. We had a meeting of seventy-two musicians in February, which succeeded in getting union action against the Case Bill, one of the first of the anti-union measures that proliferated in Congress as the war came to an end. We also came up with a program having several goals:

- A campaign for municipal support of musical activities
- A state Fine Arts Bill
- Increasing jobs for musicians through local and national union projects to "meet the needs of people in other unions, mass organizations, civic and cultural groups.

By April we had an extensive phone tree going to insure a quorum at the coming union meeting, where this program—now including opposition to another anti-union bill, the Lea Bill—would be brought to the floor. The Lea Bill was specifically aimed at the Musicians' Union, and came to be referred to as the "Anti-Petrillo Law." (James Petrillo was president of the AFM from 1940 to 1958.)

Within the orchestra, the few Communists and other progressives were also active in proposing improvements in the contract for the following season. In the spring, as the season neared its end, orchestra meetings were held. Opinion coalesced around a demand for "90 and 25"—a ninety dollar a week minimum salary and a twenty-five week season.

As personnel manager, Charles White usually did not attend these meetings. He always knew what went on, however, and warned some of the more vocal members of the orchestra, "You had better be mighty careful what you do at that meeting."

Although his truthful testimony to the union board had helped me secure my position in the orchestra, I had soon found that he was very much a management man. He enjoyed calling the conductor "Wally" and looked on him as the captain of the ship. He considered it his job to keep any musician from rocking the boat. He was a performer—a kettle drum man—and not only a member of the union but presumably a union steward. That was an impossible combination.

When the president and vice president of the Local Union came to discuss contract proposals with the musicians, White did attend. His presence cast a pall over the discussion. He gave his opinion freely afterward: "If the minimum goes up to ninety it will probably be necessary to cut ten or twenty off the roster. Naturally, the management, if it is going to spend that much, will look for better men. We can expect a great number of auditions this summer."

In conversations among the musicians after the meeting, a number of us found that we had a similar feeling of dissatisfaction. There had not been an adequate opportunity to get over to our union officials what we wanted in negotiations, nor did we understand their position clearly. So seven of us went to see President Wallace at the union office: Alex Walden, Edgar Roemheld and myself from the bass section, violinist Isabelle Daskoff, cellist Harold Schneir, horn player Harry Parshall, and first clarinetist Kalman Bloch.

White actually called the union while we were there to find out who was participating. Although the union did not tell him, he soon found out. Shortly thereafter, the list of orchestra members who would have additional work in recording sessions was posted. Only one of the seven was included.

Bloch was a key player who could hardly be omitted. The others, though not holding first chair positions, were well up in their sections and/or had participated in previous recordings, so there was no musical justification for their omission. An enlarged Orchestra Committee meeting was held. White was called to account. As a result, the three most obvious cases of discrimination were rectified.

In the meantime, an even more serious matter of discrimination had surfaced but had not been mentioned at the Committee meeting. During a rehearsal recess, White had been shuffling papers at the podium as he talked with some of his friends. He showed them a short, unsigned note, saying it was from Wally. The note ordered him to hire "No more Jews, Italians or women."

The stir that resulted brought the note to the attention of some he would certainly have preferred should know nothing about it. I was outraged. We had just fought a war against anti-Semitic fascism and here it was appearing casually on our own stage. Adding sexism and discrimination against Italians made it all the worse.

At the next orchestra meeting, on April 4, I blasted the policy, White by name and the conductor by implication. I expected others who had seen the note to speak out when I had broken the ice. It didn't happen. There was certainly a commotion, but no overt support.

That evening, when I reported for the concert, I was turned away by Wilfrid Davis, the Associate Manager, with no explanation except that "We were sorry for what you did this afternoon."

I was not allowed to play the last two weeks of the season although, in accordance with my contract, I was paid for those weeks. When the union subsequently requested a written statement, Davis wrote that the reason I was not allowed to play was that "Mr. White would not go on stage and play the performance if Mr. Russell Brodine were allowed to play because Mr. Brodine had made certain statements and allegations against Mr. Wallenstein and against Mr. White."

White denied that there was any intent to discriminate against anyone and circulated a letter through the orchestra for signatures stating that the signers had no knowledge of any discrimination.

We held an emergency meeting of my Communist Club. I realized by this time that I should have consulted with my comrades and with my colleagues, especially those who were already on the firing line with me over the recording list, before making that speech. Consulting together now, we concluded that it would be impossible to pursue the matter of the general discriminatory policy. It was being denied. We had no proof. Undoubtedly, the damning evidence of the note had been destroyed. Although we were sure it had come from Wallenstein we did not know whether he instigated it or whether it had come from someone on the Symphony Board.

We hoped that having it made known to the orchestra and the union would make it more difficult to put such a policy into practice. Had it become known to the Symphony Board, Wallenstein would certainly have been in trouble, as there were Jews on that Board. (It was a shock to me many years later to see Wallenstein listed as one of many Jewish musicians of accomplishment. I had not known that he was a German Jew and regarded his attitude to the musicians as typically Prussian.)

We came up with a well-documented case against White for actions in violation of the union constitution throughout the season, culminating in my dismissal. I filed charges against him with the union a few weeks later.

Subsequently, he charged me with a campaign of slander and distortion against him that was detrimental to his interests and standing as a steward and to his relationship with Wallenstein. I was already out of a job. If his charges had been substantiated, I could have been out of the union and for all practical purposes, out of the profession.

There were some tense times before the dust of that fight settled. I lost a lot of sleep and I'm sure other musicians did, too. Virginia and I, however, always managed to squeeze some humor out of even the most dismal situation.

"At least," I said to her, "at the very least, we have each other." We called it our minimum program. Through the years, there were many times of stress: too much work, too little money, personal and political disappointments. At such times, we always reminded one another of our "minimum program," got a laugh out of it and a second wind for the next problem.

The upshot of the Los Angeles struggle was that White remained in the orchestra but lost his position as personnel manager and as union steward and was fined for his handling of my dismissal. Nothing came of his charges against me. I had too much support in the orchestra, and Charley had too little to make a case.

Nevertheless, I was out of a job. None of the other musicians in that group of seven were rehired the following year either, except Bloch, who was indispensable.

"90 and 25" were not won in the orchestra's contract for the following year, but they did get a raise in the minimum from eighty to eighty-five. Five additional weeks were proposed, but not guaranteed—they were optional to management.

These events taught me an important lesson about building an organized, collective struggle around any issue. Going out on a limb alone or as one of a few can make it possible for management to chop off the limb, resulting in lost jobs and setting the struggle back, at least for a time. It didn't mean I would ever give up on union principles nor would I give up on fighting injustice. What I learned was to struggle—not alone, but together with others; not to become impatient, but to develop strategy and tactics collectively.

Even to struggle in my chosen profession, however, I had to have a job. Obviously, I was unlikely ever to play in the Los Angeles Philharmonic again. My studio work was hardly enough to live on and in any case was not musically satisfying most of the time. My arrest on the Craft Guild picket line was enough to make film jobs sparse while my fight in the Symphony and my vocal participation in union meetings tended to cause contractors for other jobs to look upon me as a troublemaker.

It was a peculiarity of our union that most contractors who did the hiring of musicians came out of the ranks of performers and retained their membership in the union. Besides having a conflict of interest, they were always privy to what went on in union meetings and who the most militant union members were.

Kendall's husband was back from his wartime stint in the merchant marine by this time and all three of the Fraziers went back to Seattle, leaving additional room in our big house.

We made a separate apartment on our second floor for Alice and Nemmy Sparks. Nemmy was the new District Organizer for the Party in Southern California. It wasn't easy for someone in his position to find pleasant accommodations, and the rent helped make our house payments.

Both of them became attached to Cynthia, whose bedtime routine came to include a goodnight kiss for each of them.

The light opera summer season at the Greek Theater was my most substantial job during this period. It helped financially, but for one awful moment I thought it had destroyed my instrument.

One of the operas has a scene in which the villain has the rest of the cast lined up across the stage while he threatens them with a large, theatrical, old-fashioned pistol. One hot, damp summer night, he swung the pistol from one side of the line-up to the other. It slipped out of his hand, sailed through the air down into the orchestra pit, and smack into my bass, crushing the top.

I don't think I could have felt much worse if it had struck *me*. Fortunately, an instrument repairman did an excellent job of restoring the bass, and the company paid for the repairs. It served me well for many more years.

While working that job, I would get home at midnight, then have to get up at five o'clock to take care of Cynthia. Virginia suffered from asthma all her life and was having a serious problem with it that summer. She could function during the day, but breathing was difficult in the nights and early mornings. Cynthia chose that time to begin waking up at dawn.

In the fall of 1946, somewhat to our surprise, I received a contract as principal bass in Salt Lake City for the 1946-47 season. It came through Phil Kahgan, the contractor from whom I got what studio work came my way. I had looked on Kahgan as a parasite like most contractors, getting everything he could out of both studios and musicians and accepting "gifts" from the latter who hoped to get jobs through him, or were thanking him for his calls. I had never participated in those kickbacks, yet throughout this and succeeding years, when no one else would hire me, he continued to call me and other left-wing musicians.

WHERE NEXT?

The trip to Salt Lake City proved to be the first of several that took us to western orchestras in the next few years, although Los Angeles remained our home base. Cynthia—or Dinny, as we called her then—became an experienced traveler.

Driving through Montana in a high wind, the roof of our old '34 Chevrolet blew off. Dinny hung her doll's clothes over the exposed slats and enjoyed sticking her hand up between them to wave at the engineers of passing trains.

On another of those ex-

Cynthia playing the bass

peditions, she asked, "When we've been everywhere, then where will we go?"

The Utah Symphony was new, established as a division of the Utah State Institute of Fine Arts, supplemented with private funding. The Mormon Tabernacle Choir had given the city a reputation in the field of vocal music, but instrumental music had been lacking. The orchestra had only sixty-eight members, the bass section, five. Three were local bassists, none of whom had adequate training or experience, though one had real possibilities. He took a few lessons from me, and I believe went on to a professional career in another city.

Although this was not my first experience as a principal, the responsibility here was heavier than ever before. David Gangursky, the other experienced bassist from out of town, and I had to carry the bass part, bringing the others along as best we could. It wasn't easy, but I came away from it with increased confidence, finding that I had overcome the pre-concert nerves of the past.

Werner Janssen was the conductor. His ambitions were bigger than his abilities, and like many people who want to be accepted as more than they are, he was afraid to admit mistakes. Since I had played under him in Los Angeles, I knew what to expect—not much in any case, and here he had fewer experienced musicians to help him along. When he corrected an orchestra member he would sometimes beat his chest and say, "What if *I* should make a mistake?"

This was a State Orchestra, so we did a lot of touring to small towns around Utah, usually playing in Mormon District Community Centers—called Stake Houses—or in high school gyms. Sometimes a big clock on a Stake House wall would bong out the hour in the midst of a symphony.

When we rehearsed in the Mormon Tabernacle, we often had to pause while a group of tourists were brought in to observe the famous acoustics. They would be placed in the rear of the hall while the guide went far forward and dropped a pin so they could hear how remarkably the sound carried. The pin was more substantial than an ordinary head pin, however, leading to jokes among the musicians about whether he was using a nail or a railroad spike.

On tour we played a short piece by Jarnfeldt as an encore. The first time we played it, Janssen gave one more dramatic beat after the music ended. He looked rather foolish, and was obviously upset.

Calling the percussion man over after the concert, he demanded, "Why didn't you play that last note?"

"I don't have such a note." He showed Janssen his music.

"Don't tell me. I knew the composer." Janssen took the music and wrote in one more note. We had to play the piece for the rest of the tour with that ridiculous tail tacked on to the end.

Musical matters were shadowed that year by the devastating change in the political atmosphere. The reactionary offensive had begun even before the war ended. Any illusions we had entertained of continued national unity after the war were long gone. The old fight of the ruling class against the people in general, labor in particular, and "Reds" most of all was back in all its old virulence, with some new wrinkles added.

We should have expected that all along. Every gain under the New Deal, every victory for organized labor in the Thirties had been won in the political arena, in the streets and on the picket lines in battles against capitalist companies, in mass pressure on the Roosevelt administration. And now we had a military-industrial complex that had gained wealth and power during the war and had no intention of relinquishing it. What made 1947 such a painful year was less the attack from the Right than the way the resistance to it seemed to shrink from day to day.

New Deal policies were betrayed by formerly liberal Democrats, labor unity was disrupted by formerly progressive union leaders. Public figures who—pro-capitalist though they might be—had spoken out for living together in the same world with socialist countries, now enlisted in the Cold War against the Soviet Union. Anti-Communism, which had been somewhat in remission during the wartime alliance, was now becoming a cancerous growth.

Paul Robeson came to Salt Lake City on what proved to be his last major concert tour. His appearance on the University campus was sponsored by the American Student Union chapter, among others. Hate groups worked to torpedo the concert, labeling the great singer himself and the ASU "red."

Although the concert went on, the campus credentials of the ASU were revoked. On the concert stage, Robeson spoke words of encouragement and support for the students, but free speech suffered a defeat on that campus, as on many others.

1947 was indeed a bad year for the country. President Truman instituted loyalty oaths for government employees, the Attorney General published a list of "subversive organizations," the Taft-Hartley Act reversed many of the gains for union organization established in 1935 by the Wagner Act. Taft-Hartley required union leaders, too, to swear that they were not now and had never been Communists or any other kind of "subversive."

The House Un-American Activities Committee, which had been turned into a standing committee of the House, embarked on a headline-grabbing witch-hunt in Hollywood. Senator Joseph McCarthy was not yet on the scene, but what came to be known as "McCarthyism" was well underway.

Living in a conservative city far from the big, vital progressive movement of which we had been a part for the previous ten years, and living in Utah too short a time to become integrated into local struggles, it seemed to us that everything had changed between October of 1946 and April of 1947. When we got back to Los Angeles in the spring we were swept up briefly in the organized fight-back against these reactionary measures, but we were there only a couple of months. I was offered a summer job in the Central City Opera Company in Colorado—again through Phil Kahgan.

The preliminary rehearsals were in Denver, so we stayed there with Virginia's father and stepmother, then occupied their mountain cabin between Denver and Central City during the performances.

I enjoyed playing opera again, the first time since my season with the Philadelphia Opera Company. The bass section has a little different role in an opera orchestra than in a symphony, an important role in providing firm support for the singers.

Emile Cooper, a Metropolitan Opera conductor, was conducting. My stand partner was Ed Arian, whom I had known slightly in Philadelphia. We got along well both musically and personally.

After the first concert, the critics complained that the orchestra was drowning out the singers. The criticism was well taken. Throughout rehearsals and at that first concert Cooper had asked for more and more bass and we had given him what he wanted. At the second concert, he tried to make it clear that it had not been his fault the orchestra was too loud. He not only motioned for the basses to play softer, but used insulting and exaggerated gestures to indicate that we were the ones who had been responsible.

During intermission, Ed and I agreed to play just loud enough to hold the opera together. Cooper signaled for more bass, but we continued to play softly—not enough to injure the performance, just enough to teach him a lesson. The concertmaster told us later that as Cooper continued to ask for more with no response from us, he cursed in several languages.

After the second intermission, we responded to the conductor's directions, giving him what he asked for. We got along fine with him after that. Respect has to flow both ways between conductor and musicians to make good music.

Ed had been principal bass in the Denver Symphony, but he and a few others had been pushing for better pay and had not been rehired for the coming season. He was returning to Phila-

delphia where he was to begin a twenty-year stint in the Philadelphia Orchestra.

Ed played an important role in improving conditions in that
orchestra, too. After leaving it he wrote two books on the subject of the organization and support of symphonies and other
art organizations.[7] Ed's address to the 1992 ICSOM Conference
was both a chapter in symphony history and an assessment of
the current situation for orchestra musicians.[8]

Ed urged me to audition for his Denver job so I arranged to
play for Saul Caston, the conductor. Caston seemed favorably
impressed, but the personnel manager, Harry Safstrom, was
not eager to have me in the section. He had been a bass student at Curtis when I was there but was neither an outstanding musician nor a friend.

So Denver was out, and I had heard nothing about a second
season in Utah. We decided to visit the family in Seattle, stop-
ping on the way in Salt Lake.

Ross Beckstead, the Utah personnel manager, met us in a
cafe for a cup of coffee. He assured me that he would like to
have me back. There was no criticism of my playing nor of my
leadership of the section. He hemmed and hawed and finally
said, "Russell, if you would just straighten yourself out with
the FBI, I could give you a contract tomorrow."

Straighten myself out with the FBI? Abandon my principles
and join the slimy "witnesses" who were naming names and
telling lies about their former friends and comrades? I would
never have been straight again.

Losing the Salt Lake job proved to be no sacrifice. I kept in
touch with Kahgan, of course, and learned that Janssen was
not returning to Utah. He was to conduct the Portland, Oregon
orchestra, which was being revived after an interval of nearly
ten years. I was offered the first chair in the bass section at
$130 a week for 21 weeks, one week longer and $5 more than
in Utah.

The FBI probably contacted the management of the Portland
Orchestra, too, but if so, Manager Philip Hart had the courage
to hire me anyway.

Perhaps the FBI was just using different tactics. When we
got to Portland we stopped in at the Party office. The District
Organizer asked if I had a friend by the name of Taylor. I couldn't
recall such a person.

"That's what I suspected," he said. "Someone called here and said he was 'Taylor,' an old friend of yours, and wanted to know if I could give him your address."

I doubt if "Taylor" expected any information. He certainly got none. Apparently, the tactic was to scare me by letting me know I was being watched. While we were in Portland, whenever we found ourselves being closely followed by another car, one of us would say, "There's Taylor again."

Janssen was no better in Portland than he had been in Salt Lake, but there were more experienced musicians and a slightly larger orchestra. Some had played in the Portland Symphony in its previous incarnation, and Portland had a Junior Symphony which had given others training and experience. Portland prided itself on being the "Boston of the West" and in fact, had a longer and more varied history of musical culture than Salt Lake.

Again there were first chair players from Los Angeles or elsewhere to supplement the local talent. In both cities, the local people were glad to have the musical reinforcements, yet the "imports" had to be paid more, which led to some resentment. There was less friction in Portland over this, which made for pleasanter relationships.

The first fiddles on one side and the twelve-person cello section on the other occupied the front of the stage. The first time I saw those cellos I couldn't believe the seating arrangement: six men on the outside, six women on the inside. There could be no purpose for such a configuration except the desire to hide the women behind the men, a kind of apology for being forced to hire women, a weird example of refusing to accept them on a basis of equality.

When the season was over, I asked for a raise for the following year. As soon as wartime price controls were removed, prices had soared. I had the additional cost of moving my family twice a year and finding housing in Portland, not easy since the wartime housing shortage had not yet eased. The contract I was offered not only did not include a raise; it cut me back to $125 a week.

It seemed unlikely that the Symphony Association could find any other qualified bass player to accept that salary for the first chair position, so although I returned to Los Angeles without a contract for the 1948-49 season, I expected to continue negotiating, and eventually get a reasonable offer. In the end, Steven

Mala, who had been my stand partner, was moved up to principal at the lower pay, and I was again out of a job.

We were in Los Angeles for an entire year this time. It was our economic low point. During the previous few years, studio music had been consolidated in such a way that there was much less freelance work. In addition, the unacknowledged blacklist was hurting other progressive musicians as well as myself.

From the spring of 1948 to the fall of 1949, I had only five checks for music jobs for a total of $756, and at least one of those checks was not for a new job, but for a "residual." The union had recently won a fight for residual pay for musicians when a recording they had made was reused.

Comrades in the building trades came to my rescue, finding me a job on a crew that was putting up a small commercial building and getting me into the Carpenters' Union. Although nationally that union was bureaucratic and business-union oriented, Local 634 had democratically-elected, progressive leadership. My participation in the CSU Carpenters' picket line had established my credentials.

My amateur carpentering had not prepared me for the real world of construction. I could pound nails, but my new co-workers could see that when I got much beyond that I didn't know my ass from my elbow. Besides, although music is hard work, requiring intense concentration, it is not muscle-building, so I was also ill prepared for the less skilled but more physically demanding of the tasks.

The building was framed in when I was told to move a pile of wet planks twelve feet long, twelve inches wide and two inches thick from the ground to the second floor. I picked each one up, leaned it against the skeleton wall, pushed it higher, and with a final lunge, sent it on to the floor above. With each plank it became more difficult. After half an hour or forty-five minutes, I couldn't manage that final lunge—the plank would come back at me. The foreman saw my difficulty and gave me something else to do. I got a lot of instruction and a lot of help; more than one mistake was forgiven.

I may not have been much of an asset on the job, but my comrades and their allies in the union were glad to have one more man in their progressive caucus. A faction in the union, allied with the reactionary international leadership, was carrying on a fight to unseat the elected officers of the Local. Union meetings were stormy. The right-wing faction had once tried to take over the union hall by force.

We feared they might try again during the Christmas holidays, when presumably we would be celebrating. We divided our forces into groups of perhaps half-a-dozen each to guard the hall.

I was on the Christmas Eve team. I don't recall that night well, except that we had doors and windows locked and barred and were armed with short lengths of pipe in case of invasion. Had there been trouble, I probably would not have been much more effective than when I "helped" to break down the gates at the Philadelphia City Hall. Fortunately, the night was quiet. At dawn we turned over the guard duty to another shift and headed home.

I began to realize that it really was Christmas and I had no gift for my little daughter. Catching sight of a floral shop just opening for the Christmas trade, I stopped and bought her a bouquet. She was thrilled to get such a grown-up present.

The opposition to the Democratic Party's move to the right had coalesced by this time in the Progressive Party and the candidacy of Henry Wallace for President. He had been Secretary of Agriculture and then Vice President under FDR. His campaign in 1948 was a spirited one.

Not long after we returned to L.A., we attended a Wallace meeting. The numbers and the enthusiasm were exciting. There were film celebrities on the program, some making big donations.

Katherine Hepburn spoke, and not merely as a performer reading a script. She wrote and spoke what she believed. Yet it was only a one-night stand for her. As she describes it in her autobiography, she didn't ask L. B. Mayer, the head of her studio, MGM, for permission to make the speech. He would have denied it, and she would have done it anyway.

Yet she acknowledges his "right" to put limitations on her freedom of speech. She says she told him he had "a perfect right not to pay me a weekly salary from here on in" because "I have done something that an employee of a large institution has no right to do."[9]

Judging by her later absence from the fight against McCarthyism, she preferred keeping her career in that "large institution" humming along without any further challenges to her boss's "rights."

The Wallace campaign had a significant effect. It forced Truman, in a tight race against Thomas Dewey, to woo former Democrats back by taking over some of the main planks of the Progressive platform on domestic issues.

Fearing a Republican win, many Wallace supporters switched at the last minute and voted for Truman. We saw it in our own precinct. We had canvassed the neighborhood and were convinced Wallace would get a respectable number of votes. I was a poll watcher and saw that expected number cut to less than half. Nationally, there weren't the votes we had hoped for to lay the basis for a strong third party.

During the summer before the election, twelve national leaders of the Communist Party were indicted under the Smith Act, a law passed in 1940 to make it possible to prosecute people who advocated socialism solely for their beliefs. It had been almost forgotten during the war. Now the CP leaders were charged with "conspiracy to teach and advocate the duty and necessity to overthrow the U.S. government by force and violence."

Both the wording of the Act and the way it was prosecuted were unconstitutional, but it was nine years before the Supreme Court reversed the decisions against the Communists. Charges were then dropped against those awaiting trial. Meanwhile, those convicted had spent years in jail, and the highly publicized trials had contributed to the muzzling of free speech and the anti-Communist hysteria of that decade.

During that period, some secondary Party leaders went underground in order not to allow the Party to be completely beheaded. In retrospect, it is generally agreed that this was a mistake, but at the time, with the sad history of the German Party still fresh, it did not seem unreasonable. There had been a large, vital Communist Party in Germany when Hitler came to power. The Party attempted to continue its legal activities after the attacks against Communists began and was decimated by the Nazis.

Two of those who were to drop from sight were Nemmy and Alice Sparks. After they left our home, but before they left the area, we had one last meal together in a restaurant, and said good-bye. That was a bad moment. The chill of fascism was touching us on that warm California street as we watched them drive away. We didn't see them again for seven years.

After they left, we divided up our house into separate apartments and rooms and filled it with friends and comrades. Their rent helped keep us afloat.

As the fall of 1949 and a new symphony season approached, a musical opportunity opened once more. Edgar Lustgarten, who had been principal cellist in St. Louis, moved to Hollywood, bringing with him a commission from the St. Louis conductor, Vladimir Golschmann, to fill a vacancy in the bass section. No audition would be necessary; Golschmann trusted his judgment. Ed offered me the job. Our travel expenses would be reimbursed when we got to St. Louis, but we were so broke we didn't have travel money. Our renters all pitched in and paid enough rent in advance to get us to St. Louis, besides giving us a farewell dinner and parting gifts.

ST. LOUIS: THE FIRST SEASON

One of our African-American friends, Myrtle Pitts, who had lived in St. Louis for a few years during the depression, warned us that it was "a northern city with a southern exposure." Myrtle was a social worker who had grown up in Salem, Oregon, and graduated from the University of Oregon. She had been offered a job in St. Louis and had assumed she could do graduate work at Washington University. Not only was she barred from that University, she experienced more discrimination than she had ever known in Oregon and was appalled at the conditions under which her African-American clients had to live.

On our way to the new job, Virginia and I talked about living in a segregated city. We were determined that we were not going to live segregated lives. There would never be a party in our house that was all white. We would make sure our daughter was not disadvantaged by having only white playmates.

We entered Missouri from the south in early October. The days were sunny; the trees on the rolling hills were full of color. We had a favorable impression of the state that was to be our home for almost thirty years.

We announced our entrance to St. Louis in a way that turned heads to look at our passing. The rear end of our old '34 Chevrolet was threatening to drop out. It sounded more like a cement mixer than a passenger car. We thought it had come to the end of its road. Fortunately, considering the state of our finances, we were able to replace the rear end and keep it going a few more years.

The postwar housing shortage made it difficult to find a place to live. This was particularly true for a couple with a small child. My stand partner, June Rotenberg, an old acquaintance from Philadelphia, came up with a solution. She knew an artist who had just received a Fulbright fellowship to study abroad and would be giving up his studio. We were able to take his place.

Our new home was a big, barn-like, high-ceilinged space on the lower floor of an old hotel near the riverfront. The hotel, once a fashionable place when the riverfront was the center of city life, was now a rundown establishment occupied mainly by old men on pensions. We were in a warehouse district, perfumed by a Tums factory nearby, but we had a good neighbor next door in Bill Fett, an artist who taught at Washington University.

The previous tenant had made partitions between "rooms" with some of the tall shutters that were typical of old St. Louis houses, and had relieved the gloom—there was only one storefront-type window in front—by painting the lower eight feet of the walls in bright colors. Dark red calcimine that had once been applied to the ceiling was now flaking off, which provided a favorite game for Cynthia. The three of us would lie on our backs on the bed in the dark, sending the beam of a flashlight up to find pictures in the weird shapes on the ceiling.

June was a frequent visitor, having adopted Cynthia as her little sister. June was amused by the tall, black, old-fashioned stove, and she highlighted its name with aluminum paint so it announced in brilliant letters that we had a "Radiant Home."

Our place was also variously dubbed "The Show Place of Lower Clark Street" or "Big Bohemia,"—mimicking "Little Bohemia," the bar on the corner. Being within walking distance of the Civic Auditorium where the Symphony played made our "radiant home" a great place for after-concert parties and other gatherings.

It was not a choice neighborhood for a five-year-old girl, but Cynthia enjoyed walks along the river. We soon found her a place to spend a few hours each day in a pre-school program at an interracial settlement house not far away.

Before the season was over, we had made what proved to be lifelong friendships with Henry Loew, who joined the orchestra that same year, and with the Ormond and Goldsmith families who had come a season or two earlier. Ed Ormond is a violist with a lifelong love affair with music and with his Czech wife, Mimi. He is well organized and levelheaded and

Henry Loew, my stand partner in the St. Louis Symphony for 23 years

played an important role in the organizing of the orchestra. The following season Newton Pacht joined the bass section and also became a lifelong friend.

After knocking around from shipyard to music to carpentry and from L.A. to Salt Lake to Central City to Portland, the season in the St. Louis Symphony was delightful.

Golschmann, the conductor, had spent many years in Paris and was particularly fond of the French classics. Although I grew somewhat tired of *La Valse* and *La Mer* in subsequent years, they were a pleasure initially.

Golschmann had the ability to get the orchestra to produce a lush sound. When he was dissatisfied he would not groan and say "Jesus Christ!" like Wallenstein. Instead, he would tell us "Do somesing!" and we would, indeed, do something. Although his beat was hard to follow, I soon became accustomed to his technique.

St. Louis had one of the oldest orchestras in the country, with good and experienced musicians. I was in a bass section that was ready to accept any musical challenge that came along. I had a fine stand partner in June. She was a sensitive and dramatic artist.

Our season ended with an eastern tour, climaxed by a Carnegie Hall concert. Although Golschmann assured us this was just another concert, we rehearsed Mozart's 40th Symphony so much that we called it "Mozart's New York Symphony" thereafter.

Everywhere on the tour, audiences responded with enthusiasm and standing ovations. Virgil Thomson, composer and music critic for the *New York Times,* called the Carnegie Hall concert "one of the most delightful of the season" and the orchestra a "well-trained group, sensitive as to nuance and rich of tone." [10]

Although Golschmann generally had a good rapport with the orchestra, not all was smooth in the conductor-orchestra relationship. At the beginning of one rehearsal, late in the season, Golschmann told the musicians he had talked with members of the Board who wanted to cut salaries for the following season. He claimed to have insisted that salaries not be cut, although they could hardly be raised, as the union was asking. He concluded by raising his baton to begin rehearsing.

I interrupted. "Mr. Golschmann," I said, "you have had your say on this matter. Let us have ours." That initiated a brief discussion. The outcome of the negotiations with the Symphony

Board was that the musicians did get a few dollars more, and as we later learned, Golschmann got a $5,000 raise.

At the end of the season Henry Loew was made principal, and I was moved up to assistant principal. Although I already respected Henry as a musician and liked him as a person, I could hardly know then what an important step that was in my life. For twenty-three years we were stand partners. We stood side-by-side, sharing the same music stand, playing off the same music. As we came to know one another, each could sense the other's response to the music. There were times, however, when a conductor who fussed and fussed would get on Henry's nerves. Finally, he would lean over to me and say admiringly, "He's such a perfectionist! He's a perfect ass."

Another example of Henry's cool head and sometimes humorous leadership came when a well-known conductor arrived from Vienna for a week of rehearsals and concerts. I was excited, as he had an impressive reputation. We were not disappointed. However, in rehearsal at one point he stopped, pointed to the basses and asked for more volume. We produced more. Not satisfied, he wanted more. About five or six times: "More, more, more!" Henry Loew at this time whispered to me, "Next time around, raise your eyebrows. Pass the word along." We did so. The conductor blew us a magnificent kiss.

We were on the first stand that gave the lead to the bass section, so this rapport between us was important to the whole section and the orchestra.

Henry and I were stand partners in another sense. We stood by each other. When either of us stood up for the needs and rights of the musicians, the other stood beside him.

After our previous experience with the FBI, Virginia and I had held our breath to see whether this would be another case of one season and out. Not at all. The contract that gave me the assistant principal chair also gave me a raise from $82.50 to $95.00 a week. After such a musically satisfying season, it didn't seem too important that it lasted only twenty-three weeks. My chances for supplementary work would be as good as in Los Angeles and probably better.

Cynthia would be old enough to start kindergarten in the fall of 1950 and deserved to live in one place throughout her school years. We wanted another child, too, but had postponed increasing the family while our lives were so unsettled.

We returned to Los Angeles only to sell our house and ship what possessions were worth moving to our new home.

Our L.A. years ended in grim days. One of the memorable episodes of that summer was the demonstration at the airport when good-byes were said to the "Hollywood Ten" when they went off to serve their year in jail. These were the courageous writers and directors who had defied the House Un-American Activities Committee and stood on their First Amendment rights to be silent in the face of accusations and harassment.

That same summer the Korean War began. As in the Gulf War of 1991, the United States pulled a number of countries together under the aegis of the United Nations to fight that war. This was possible in 1950 because the Soviet Union had walked out of the Security Council in protest against putting the Taiwan government instead of Communist China in the seat reserved for China by the UN charter. The Soviet Union returned to the Security Council, and not until 1991, when there was no Soviet Union to oppose imperialist adventures, did such U.S. use of the United Nations again become possible.

The war—or the "UN police action" as it was then called—brought with it a new rash of efforts to silence the Communist Party and other voices for peace and democracy. Municipal ordinances were passed in a number of cities, including L.A., outlawing the Party. In a midnight sweep, twenty-one Los Angeles Party leaders were arrested and jailed. It was rather quickly recognized that municipalities did not have the power to take citizenship rights away from people. The city had to let the Reds go.

Nevertheless, as we drove first north to visit the family in Seattle, and then east to St. Louis, we stopped frequently to pick up newspapers, fearing the worst. It was both frustrating but also, in a way, reassuring that most of the local dailies seemed little concerned with either the war or anti-communism.

Once in St. Louis, things seemed much as when we left. We wondered then, and often afterward, why I was able to remain on the job while McCarthyism took a toll of Communists and progressive unionists in every field, including music. I never knew until many years later that the FBI had regularly checked on me with the personnel managers. Although I had my differences with those in charge of hiring and firing, sometimes sharp differences, I credit them with putting music first. As long as I performed well as a musician, they were not going to fire me simply because the FBI had me on its list.

We were also lucky in the timing of our move. When a St. Louis stoolpigeon named names before a House Un-American Activities Committee hearing, I had not been in town long enough to get on his list. And when a stoolpigeon in Los Angeles named Communist musicians before the House Un-American Activities Committee, I had been gone long enough that he had apparently forgotten me. As will be seen later, the FBI made itself felt in our lives, but we escaped the kind of public pillorying that destroyed so many careers during those years.

LIVING IN ST. LOUIS

After our second season in St. Louis, Virginia and I began to house hunt. We were not alone in that project. We had Walter and Essie Johnson as partners and were looking for a house that could, with some work, accommodate both families.

We first encountered Walter Johnson in February 1950, when we attended a Negro History Week observance in one of the African-American churches. One of the scheduled speakers failed to appear and Walter was called on to take his place. On the spur of the moment he made one of the most powerful and eloquent speeches we had ever heard. Its theme was "If you want to stand up, you can stand up anywhere."

He illustrated that theme with a story from his childhood in Louisiana when his father, his mother and he—a youngster of about twelve—held off a lynch mob.

Virginia got acquainted with Essie the following year when she was hired to help with housework. Both Walter and Essie were helpful to her and Cynthia while I was on a lengthy tour. The Johnsons, like the Brodines, needed a better place to live. The two women conceived the idea of finding a joint dwelling. If we pooled our money, we could do better than either family alone.

The first night after my return, the four of us had dinner together to discuss the idea. We decided to put it into practice at once. It was a Saturday night. We bought a Sunday paper and started our hunt then and there.

We wanted a duplex or an old house that could be made into a duplex so that each family could have its own apartment. In the succeeding weeks we found more than one place that looked promising, but we ran into an obstacle: No one wanted to sell to such an unusual combination of buyers. We looked at houses in areas where whites were moving out and blacks were moving in, so we did not expect the problems with racism we would have had in all-white areas.

Our partnership apparently looked like a poor risk to real estate agents. They found it unbelievable that such a combination could survive. They were willing to sell to either blacks or whites in one of these "changing" neighborhoods—one duplex we wanted but couldn't get was sold to two African-American brothers—but an integrated household was too unusual.

The next time we found a house all four of us liked, we tried a new tactic. Virginia and I bought the house and sold a half interest to Walter and Essie. The original contract was on one or two long sheets of paper and in very small print. We were very suspicious that there might be a clause that would prohibit us from selling to our new African-American partners. We had arrived at the real estate office shortly before quitting time, and the realtor was biting his fingernails. He couldn't understand why we didn't just sign and let him go home to his nice hot dinner. We persisted—the contract was OK. We penned our names. He sure slammed the door on the way out.

We moved into our home at 4757 Labadie Avenue in early September 1951.

Essie and Walter Johnson, our living partners
from 1951 until their deaths

Contrary to the predictions of the real estate agents, we developed our own enduring small caring community, which endured for nearly fifty years. We lost Walter, who died in 1990, but the other three of us remained together until Essie's death in 1999.

The Labadie house had been a single-family dwelling, so at first we all had to share kitchen and bathroom. I got busy making a kitchen out of one of the bedrooms in what would be our apartment on the second floor. The following summer, I added another bedroom by building an extension out over the downstairs back porch. Essie got her brother's help to put in a downstairs bathroom.

Cynthia had seldom had a playmate when we lived in the warehouse district. She was happy with our new home and was soon playing with the neighborhood children. We had a Halloween party to which we invited them all, including one little white girl about Cynthia's age who was not allowed to play with the black children.

When Virginia and Cynthia carried the invitation to this child's home and stood talking to the mother, the little girl jumped up and down saying, "Let me go, Mama, I want to go to the party, Mama." The barrier was broken. (Years later that mother married an African-American.)

On August 18, 1952, our son, Marc, was born. Our children grew up feeling that it was natural for black and white to live together. They say they were raised on the "four parent system."

Of course there were some problems in our joint living, especially at first. For instance, Virginia would forget that it was Essie's turn to do her laundry. Essie would find the clotheslines full of diapers. Walter lost patience with my penchant for keeping things. Quite a collection was accumulating in the basement. Walter wanted to have a grand clean-up and throw-away. We solved these minor irritations on either side by talking them over in family meetings, or by leaving them alone until the sharp edges of the differences had worn off.

We had separate apartments, sharing the basement, the yard and the garage. We had separate lives, as well. The Johnsons were devout Christians. They were deeply involved in church activities at Southern Mission Baptist Church. Our Marxist philosophy and the activities of our Party were important to us. On both sides, we accepted and respected these differences, and worked together on the social and political issues on which we agreed.

Walter worked for a moving company and was as active in the Teamsters Union as I was in the Musicians Union. We often discussed union affairs. For example, I wanted to raise the demand for a paid vacation. We already had so much unpaid "vacation" that most musicians thought I was dreaming. Walter's trade was also seasonal, with long periods of unemployment in the winter. Yet he, too, was calling for paid vacations.

"If you work only half a year you should at least get half a vacation," he told me. We took that route, and won a vacation, little by little. Now musicians have year-round contracts, with a much-needed seven or eight weeks of vacation.

During our first year on Labadie, we got acquainted with Voris Dickerson, a St. Louis artist who had recently returned from New York. He was painting portraits of Toussaint L'Ouverture and Frederick Douglass to hang in the halls of the newly built L'Ouverture Elementary School. At that time, St. Louis schools were segregated by law. All the so-called Negro schools were named for African-American leaders of the past. This one was to be named for the great Haitian revolutionary. Voris arranged for Virginia to be one of the speakers at the school's dedication because of her interest in and knowledge of Negro History.

My colleague and friend Newton Pacht was taking courses in history at Washington University and was looking for something he could do in the short time before he would be returning to New York at the end of the season. He and other friends joined the Johnsons and Brodines in deciding to get the community involved in a big Negro History Week observance.

We first had to get a representative planning group organized. Voris arranged for a meeting to be held at the Royal Vagabond Club, an African-American Men's Club. We got Herman Dreer, a teacher at Harris Teacher's College known for his interest in Negro History, to chair, and sent out many invitations.

The meeting was a smashing success. Most of the leaders in the African-American community came. O. Walter Wagner, the white leader of the Metropolitan Church Federation, attended, but otherwise the white contingent was made up of a few musicians and other progressive friends. Most white St. Louisans hardly realized there was such a thing as Negro History.

Dreer was elected chairman, and Virginia secretary. We planned to ask Golschmann to schedule a work by an African-American composer for the concerts that week; to ask the Art

Museum to hang a relevant exhibit; to get books on the subject displayed in all the public libraries; and to hold a big meeting with an historian as the main speaker.

When the next issue of the *Argus*, one of the two weekly African-American papers, appeared, our great plan and its organization appeared to have been torpedoed, almost certainly by the FBI. A news story revealed that Wagner and Leo Bohanon of the Urban League had withdrawn, and that Dreer had announced that the Committee for the Observance of Negro History Week had been dissolved.

The newspaper stated that it had "learned that the injection of what was described as 'extreme left-wing' elements was the main cause for the disbanding." A column in the paper spoke of people who came in from another city with ulterior motives. Although we were not named, this was clearly leveled at us, as Dreer confirmed. Getting a job in a new city was an ulterior motive!

We were not ready to give up. Dreer had no authority to dissolve the Committee and finally agreed that if we got an observance organized, he would participate. Dr. Lorenzo Green, a professor of history at Lincoln University, was pleased to be our main speaker. Some other fine people stayed with the project as well.

The *St. Louis American*, the other African-American weekly, published an editorial castigating the faint of heart. It pointed out that the heroes in Carter Woodson's *The Negro in our History* were "once-upon-a-time left wingers who crowded out the good and safe gents and ladies of their day." Readers were reminded also of Wendell Phillips, Charles Sumner, and William Lloyd Garrison who were "so radical until some other white men in their city of Boston would not speak or associate with them."

Our meeting during Negro History Week was held in one of the major Negro churches and was well attended. One or two libraries put up exhibits, but the celebration was nothing like what it could have been without FBI interference. The original intention, for an ongoing Negro History Committee, could not be achieved.

What did last were some of the friendships made in the course of the struggle, notably with Ulysses Donaldson, an African-American educator with whom we stayed in touch until his retirement to California.

Some months later, Essie and Virginia organized a Women's Interracial Friendship Club, based in our neighborhood and drawing in women from around the area. The Club challenged the discrimination at restaurants by arranging a theater party of ten couples, half white, and half black, to attend the summer light opera in Forest Park and to eat together afterward.

As expected, our group was rejected at the restaurant where reservations had been made. The whole restaurant had tables set, with napkins very elaborately arranged at each place. After protesting to the manager we moved on (as planned) to an African-American restaurant. This restaurant was well prepared to receive us.

The Club was more successful in another endeavor. The Civic Auditorium hired only white ushers. Working with the alderman from our district, the women broke that barrier and got jobs for several young African-Americans.

This Women's Club, too, was destroyed by the FBI. Agents visited some of the African-American members and warned them that the white women were Reds who didn't go to church. Beatrice Allen was even asked to spy on us, a proposal she indignantly rejected. She told them their business was to go after such as the KKK, not after people like us.

Ms. Allen was a beautiful and dignified woman, active in her union, the Railway Clerks, and in the NAACP. She lived across the street from us. The FBI no doubt saw this as the perfect place to have a spy. Its real significance was that being close neighbors had made it possible for Bea and Virginia to become good friends.

Bea and Essie were not intimidated, but some of the other women felt they had enough problems without being persecuted for being red as well as black.

One evening when Walter drove his moving van into the barn, he was told that two men from the FBI were waiting in the office to talk to him. He changed his clothes, clocked out, walked right past them and climbed into his car. They chased after him, and motioned to him to roll down his window.

"We just want to talk to you," one said. "Just a few questions about the people who live upstairs from you."

"I'm a man of God," Walter responded. "I'll talk to you about the Lord Jesus Christ, and that's *all* I'll talk to you about." Then he rolled up his window and drove home.

Clearly, making gains in any kind of progressive activity was almost impossible in those years. Even bringing black and white people together was subversive. People like ourselves had to dig in our heels, do our best to keep things from getting worse, and bend much of our efforts toward defending those who were the most serious targets. We were fortunate in having friends like Walter, Essie, and Bea, who had such understanding and such courage.

One of the casualties of the Cold War was the left-wing culture that was so much a part of my life in the Thirties and Forties. As performing artists, musicians have the ability—and in my opinion the responsibility—to add a musical voice to the movement for a better life, for peace, civil rights and social justice.

During the first couple of seasons in St. Louis, several symphony musicians contributed their talents to chamber music concerts for the benefit of the National Council of Arts, Sciences and Professions (ASP). I had one more opportunity to play the *Trout* for a good cause.

ASP was an outgrowth of a committee with a similar name founded in 1944 in support of progressive activity in the Democratic Party. As the Democrats under Truman moved away from the program of the Roosevelt years, ASP became one of the forerunners of the Progressive Party. It maintained an independent existence and continued activity for a few years after the Wallace campaign but fell victim to the anti-Communist attacks of the House Un-American Activities Committee and the general anti-Communist hysteria.

The more vigorously people's movements develop, the more musicians are drawn to participate, both directly in their own interests and in giving such movements a cultural dimension. I knew it would happen again, but this was a dark time for these movements. It was a very dark time for our Party. Not only were national Communist leaders being sent to jail, so were secondary leaders around the country. We had a Smith Act case in Missouri. Our District Organizer, Jim Forrest, his wife Dorothy, and three others were arrested and indicted.

They were convicted, not of any crime, of course, since none had been committed and none could be proved, but of "conspiracy" to advocate and educate for the overthrow of the government. We managed to raise bail and get them out while their case was appealed. Fortunately, they never had to serve beyond that first stint in the County jail, because the banner case—for the California Smith Act victims—won on appeal.

Nevertheless, these attacks were a hard blow to our Party and to the whole progressive and trade union movement. People were afraid to participate in any activity that might be described by the government as "subversive." This fear was so prevalent that someone who circulated the Bill of Rights—the first ten amendments to the Constitution—for signatures found most people afraid to sign.

One of our favorite letters to the editor ever published appeared about this time. It was written by friends and came out in the *Post-Dispatch* on Washington's birthday. It said simply: "George Washington didn't just conspire to overthrow the government. He did it."

The Rosenberg case touched us particularly because we could feel that the Rosenbergs were much like us, not leaders, but rank and file activists with two small children. They were framed as "atom spies," tried in an atmosphere of hysteria, and executed. Their two small boys not only lost their parents but were also mistreated throughout the period of the trial. It made us fear for Marc and Cynthia.

The problem of what would happen to them if we should be arrested was compounded by the fact that almost everyone we could think of who might help was just as likely as ourselves to be victimized.

We scraped together a few hundred dollars and sent it to Virginia's conservative Republican father, with a request that he save it for any emergency that might arise from some political attack on us. We knew we could depend on him to take care of the children until we could find some other long-term solution. Fortunately, we never had to call on him for this help, and a few years later, when the McCarthyite fog began to lift, he returned the money to us, with relief.

We were just getting used to St. Louis weather when it produced one of its most dramatic demonstrations—a tornado. Actually, we slept through it, al-

Cynthia and Marc in the yard at Labadie

though it passed close by. We did not know it had happened until we got a call from friends in the suburbs checking to see if we were all right.

Another member of the orchestra didn't fare so well. Rudy Magin was a cherubic old man who had been in the second fiddle section since long before I arrived in St. Louis. His prize possession was a large music library, collected over the years.

He lived on the top floor of the Music and Arts Building, which housed many private teachers of singing and instrumental music. The tornado swept through that neighborhood, lifted the roof off the building and scattered Rudy's music in every direction. He spent two or three days combing the area, painstakingly re-collecting his music. Some of it he never recovered. Since he missed about three rehearsals, we feared for his life.

Marc as a toddler in Forest Park, St. Louis

When Marc was two years old, Virginia got a job on the regional staff of the International Ladies' Garment Workers' Union. We put Marc in an interracial nursery school, but there was no choice for Cynthia. She had to attend Benton, the all-white neighborhood school. When that was "changed over" because the neighborhood was becoming predominantly African-American, she was bussed out of the neighborhood, although two other families joined with us in trying to get our children re-enrolled at Benton.

Ironically, it was we who then put forward the advantages of the neighborhood school, which later became the rallying cry of racists. Neighborhood schools do have advantages for children, but integration has a higher value, and sometimes bussing is necessary to achieve it.

When the famous *Brown vs. Board of Education* decision finally came from the Supreme Court, declaring segregated schools unconstitutional, we looked forward to having both of our children in integrated schools. As it turned out, that took a little doing.

The St. Louis schools introduced the track system. Cynthia qualified for the highest track, for so-called gifted children. Although these gifted classes were to be in only a few schools, we assumed that Cynthia would be in the same class with the gifted children from Benton. Not so!

We checked with the Benton principal to find out who they were and called the mother of one of them, suggesting that we get our girls together before school started so they could begin to get acquainted. To our surprise, they were slated for different schools. Once again, and in spite of the Supreme Court decision, Cynthia was to go far out of the neighborhood to be in an all-white class, another example of bussing to prevent integration.

When the first day of school came, we took Cynthia to Bates, the nearby school where the gifted children from Benton were being enrolled. Fortunately, the African-American principal was sympathetic. He agreed to enroll Cynthia there while we carried on our fight with the School Board. We had to work our way up to the Superintendent before we finally got an OK for her to stay at Bates.

Some of our friends thought we were making a mistake. Although they sincerely thought they were free of racism, they knew African-American schools had suffered discrimination, so they expected them to be second rate. What they failed to realize was that so few professional fields were open to African-Americans

Russell and Marc in Forest Park

that teaching often drew very highly qualified people. There were more black teachers than white with advanced degrees in St. Louis at the time. Cynthia's teacher had a doctorate and had studied in France at the Sorbonne. She stayed in his class for two-and-a-half years.

When Marc was ready for elementary school, he attended Benton as one of the few white children there. When he reached the grade where the track system went into effect, the gifted classes to which he was assigned were integrated from the start.

Our children had as good an education as any available in St. Louis public schools. In addition they learned to consider ethnic diversity as natural and desirable.

The fact that our children got an education in an integrated setting did not mean that all St. Louis children had that advantage. Housing continued to be largely segregated. The schools followed the pattern. Although the schools were no longer segregated by law, they continued to be largely segregated in reality.

An overcrowding problem in the predominantly black schools of the central area developed in the early 1960s. The school board dealt with it at first by bussing children far out of their neighborhoods into under-utilized schools where they were often not integrated with the white student body, but kept separate. For example, at the elementary school Marc attended, one class of black students was bussed in, along with a black teacher. They attended assemblies at their "home" school and weren't allowed to participate in functions at their destination school. When all the students marched down to a nearby amusement

park for an end-of-the-year treat, the class of black students came down to the playground to watch everyone else march off, leaving them behind.

Later, the school board built supplementary plywood buildings on school playgrounds in the overcrowded schools, depriving the children of adequate play space and further perpetuating segregation. We were involved with a group that tried to deal with the overcrowding in more rational ways, which would at the same time improve integration.

Problems continued into the 1970s. One of the last things we did before leaving St. Louis was to testify in a case brought against the School Board by the NAACP over de facto segregation.

MAKING MUSIC WITH CLASS

When I signed my first—and each of my succeeding—contracts with the St. Louis Symphony Society there was no doubt in my mind that I would not only be making music with the other musicians. I would also be participating in joint action with them for the betterment of our own conditions and of the profession as a whole. It was as much a part of my life as turning up at every rehearsal and concert to play my bass and do my utmost to contribute to the highest quality of the music.

Working for improved conditions *is* working for better music. I have been asked more than once which was more important to me: the quality of musical performance and my own part in it, or the union and political activity. I do not believe the two can be separated. Poor wages and conditions make for unstable orchestras and act as constant irritants in the preparation of concerts.

Sometimes it is fun to "play" music, but always it is work and those who do it are workers. Some people, however—including some musicians—consider that because they are artists, they are completely unlike autoworkers and miners, retail clerks and truck drivers. Unlike in some ways, yes, but they share some fundamental characteristics.

In the shipyard, I was an industrial worker with thousands of co-workers. As a carpenter, I was in a skilled trade, working with only eight or ten others on each job. As a musician, I was again a skilled worker in a closely-knit group of about 90.

In spite of differences, all three occupations required a high degree of cooperation among workers—perhaps most intensely so in music, where ensemble is the basis of a good performance. In all three cases, we who were doing the work could improve our conditions only by transferring that work cooperation to cooperative organized activity for our joint betterment. That meant organization within the work group, then as part of a union local, then as part of a national union representing the whole profession.

The conditions of the work forced this understanding on the music profession a long time ago. The Musicians Union is one of the oldest unions in the country. A loose coalition of local groups called the National League of Musicians was founded in 1886 and was replaced ten years later by the American Federation of Musicians, part of the American Federation of Labor (now the AFL-CIO). The founders felt that it was necessary that "all men and women playing musical instruments and receiving pay therefore from the public must, in order to get just wages and decent working conditions, form a labor organization."[11]

One of the founding groups for the national union came from St. Louis. It had been in existence since 1885 as the Musicians' Mutual Benefit Association (MMBA) and became Local 2 of the AFM. Yet some symphony musicians, in St. Louis as elsewhere, were slow to recognize the value of unionism, almost never attending union meetings or voting in union elections.

The kind of union representation they were getting in the Forties was commensurate with their participation. When I came to St. Louis, symphony musicians were not even consulted by the union officials when contract negotiations were taking place. They did not have the power to ratify—or refuse to ratify—a contract negotiated for them by the union officers. Union officials had to be pressured both for the right kind of representation and for including the membership in decision-making.

Some first-chair players had the illusion that the financial pie was only so big, and if they worked to raise the minimum union scale they would undermine their own ability to get premium pay. They had to learn that raising the floor does not lower the ceiling—quite the contrary. Raising the minimum wage creates pressure to raise all wages.

The need for joint action is easiest for workers to see at the level of the work group, in our case, the orchestra. The symphony is usually the largest and most stable musical group in a city but seldom if ever represents a majority in a local union. Symphony musicians are outnumbered by those in jazz, rock, and other popular musical groups, plus "Saturday night musicians" who earn their living in other ways and play only occasional dance jobs or special events. Nevertheless, low pay in popular music fields can undermine the pay scales obtainable in classical music and vice versa.

One of the big differences between being a welder or a carpenter and being a musician is that in those former jobs, I was a production worker. I was one of those whose labor creates the value that is the basis of our economy. If workers stopped producing ships and building houses, digging coal and making computers, cars and clothes, telephones and TVs, food and factories, our economy would soon grind to a halt. Not so, were music to stop.

Music is essential, too, but in a different way. Without music and other art, society would be psychologically, emotionally, intellectually, and spiritually impoverished.

No matter how important music may be to the people for whom we play, musicians cannot operate in some kind of a

In costumes Virginia made for a musical-themed costume party (early 50s)

beautiful vacuum. We, too, have to work for a living. My living as a musician, like my living as a welder, depended on getting a paycheck from the people who control the money. Like steelworkers who have a constant fight against the steel corporations to raise the amount of those paychecks, we musicians have a constant fight for the same purpose—but not against a corporation.

For whom do symphony musicians work? Not, like autoworkers, for a profit-making corporation like General Motors, Ford, or Chrysler. Not even like the Hollywood musicians who work for profit-making film companies. Only when they work for a recording company do they work for a profit-making corporation and even then not directly. The service of the orchestra as a group is contracted by the symphony management to the recording company. What the musicians receive for the recording must be negotiated with the symphony management.

In a way, symphony musicians work for all the people who love music and come to hear the concerts. That is what makes our job worthwhile. But this amorphous group of music lovers is not organized or institutionalized.

In some countries, music is regarded as essential to the public and is therefore paid for by the government. State and federal subsidies have in recent years become an important part of symphony funding in our country as well. However, at no time has it been more than a part and now even that part is being drastically cut. At no time, moreover, has the control of pay and conditions been in any other hands than those of the local non-profit symphony association in each city.

Conductors and instrumentalists both are engaged in producing the best possible music. That is also the goal of the Symphony Association as a whole. These aspects of the music business tend to obscure the fact that these various participants in the enterprise have interests that diverge in important ways.

An interest in music may lead a businessman to choose leadership in the symphony association as his particular form of "civic duty," but he is not wholly disinterested. He gets a return in prestige, in social standing. He enhances the cultural attractiveness of "his" city. A symphony orchestra is one of those things that differentiates life in a city from life in a provincial town. It is essential if the city is to attract the scientific, technical and managerial talent many enterprises need.

Thus, decision-makers in symphony associations, though without a direct profit-making interest in the music, nevertheless have a business interest that sometimes, but not always, runs parallel to the interest of the musicians. The association and its board want to have a symphony, want the best music, but they want the most Bach for the buck. This is not to denigrate the sincere interest in music many have. The fact remains that the more they pay the musicians, the more money they have to raise.

These decision-makers carry in their heads a picture of how any enterprise should work, derived from their business experience. They are accustomed to thinking in terms of keeping costs down and looking at the work force as one of those costs.

The symphony association also has a proprietary interest in the symphony. In exchange for the unpaid time they put into this civic duty, they feel justified in keeping the association within their own particular upper-class elite. In spite of gestures toward other elements in the community, especially appeals for contributions, symphony associations have seldom made serious efforts to broaden the effective control of symphony matters. Government support, often urged by musicians and their union, has drawn little interest, sometimes downright hostility from symphony associations.

There is also more than a little of the patronizing attitude that musicians should be grateful to the association for creating their jobs, and therefore that the orchestra members should willingly accept pay and conditions as determined by the association.

Their hold on the purse strings is their power. The ultimate expression of this power is their ability to cancel a season or even wipe out an orchestra altogether, as has happened more than once.

For an association member or officer, music is a marginal aspect of life, but for the musicians, it is central. Music is a musician's livelihood; the existence of the symphony is a necessity. He or she cannot pay the bills without it.

Some associations may be more committed to good music than others; some may be more understanding of the needs of the musicians than others. Yet symphony music is organized, as are most aspects of our lives, in a way that reflects the class structure of our economic system.

An association, like a corporation, is not visible on the job. Day-to-day control of the workers is expressed through an immediate supervisor, in this case, the conductor. Like the instrumentalists, he must negotiate his salary with representatives of the board. He may seek to enlarge the orchestra or to pay a little more in order to obtain particularly talented musicians, and in that sense he sees costs differently from the association. Yet he has a kind of power none of the other musicians possesses. He determines the programs, supervises the audi-

tions, and has the final word in the hiring and firing of performers. In daily rehearsals and concerts, he is the boss. A boss usually acts like a boss, even when he is a member of the union, as conductors are.

Conductors once had absolute power over hiring and firing, but musicians now exert some control over both. The struggle over that power began during my day and has achieved important results since.

Like the manager of a steel plant, the conductor—manager of the music—tends to identify with society's rulers rather than society's producers. His salary level and life style separate him from the performers and bring him closer to association members. It is part of his job to socialize with them, to keep them happy with their orchestra.

The other visible boss is the one who controls not the music, but the money. This is the business manager who runs the symphony office and handles its financial affairs.

Therefore, like other workers, we musicians have arrayed against us the power of money and the power to eliminate our jobs. What we have is the power of unity and the power to strike. Symphony association leaders cannot produce concerts. Only musicians can make music, as only garment workers can make clothes, only autoworkers can make cars.

Unity within an orchestra is not easy to achieve. Recognition of the need to move together with musicians throughout the profession is still harder to achieve. Most difficult of all for musicians, as for other artists and professionals, is to understand that they are members of a class, sharing economic and political interests with workers in other fields.

Musicians have a special role to play in this regard. As performing artists, musicians have the ability and, in my opinion, the responsibility, to add a musical voice to the citizen-chorus for a better life for all the people—for peace, civil rights and social justice.

During the Thirties, I was one of many musicians performing for Republican Spain and other anti-fascist causes. Many of us also participated in demonstrations for relief, for WPA, for other needed measures in our own country. Pete Seeger, Woody Guthrie, Earl Robinson, the Weavers, and numerous others less well known gave a musical voice to rallies and other events.

During World War II, as noted, I performed for causes ranging from the *Daily People's World* to Russian War Relief. Many,

many other musicians did likewise.

Citizen action in the streets was almost totally absent during the Fifties, and the musical voice of the progressive movement was muffled. Only after the rise of the Civil Rights movement was it heard again in St. Louis.

The more vigorous the people's movements that develop, the more musicians are drawn to participate, both immediately and directly in their own interests and in giving such movements a cultural dimension. I saw it happen in the Thirties. It happened again with symphony concerts for peace and against nuclear war. It will continue to happen.

Beyond that, my vision has always been for a socialist society in which music and other aspects of culture are neither commodities for profit-makers nor toys for the rich, but part of the lives of all the people, supported by a people's government.

It all begins, in making music as in making cars, with the bread and butter issues of pay, conditions, and union participation. This was where most of my energy went, yet I would not have had the persistence through all the ups and downs if I had not had the vision of its part in a wider and deeper struggle, and ultimately in a society that will value music for its own beauty and its own meaning, and for what it can give to people.

Henry giving Marc an accordion lesson

COMMITTEES AND SUCH

My work in the St. Louis Symphony continued to be, in the main, musically satisfying. In other respects, conditions called for picking up where I left off in Los Angeles. I had not been long enough in either Salt Lake City or Portland to do more than begin to get acquainted. In St. Louis I found others as concerned as I to improve the conditions of our work.

We did not have to start by bringing our fellow workers into the union. Classical musicians were solidly in the AFM. The union policy of having union members refuse to play with non-union members made it essential for every player to have a union card.

The AFM tended, however, to be a top-down organization, neither democratic nor militant. So our first jobs were to get our colleagues more active in the union and to get the local officers more responsive to our needs.

It was clear that nothing could be accomplished until we had an orchestra committee. Now that orchestra committees are an accepted part of the scene, it may seem strange that getting one started took any effort. In fact it took two seasons—1950-51 and 1951-52—to get one established in St. Louis.

Tours provided an especially good time for talking up the need for a committee. Grievances are always aggravated on a tour, while the closeness of not only working but living and traveling together can develop solidarity. Newton Pacht was a great addition to the bass section, both musically and politically. He also had a particularly quick wit that was especially appreciated on tours. (He later retired from music and eventually became a law professor at Howard University and then an administrative judge in New York.) When we returned from one tour, Newton volunteered to take our grievances to the union.

Sam Meyers, who was then president of the Local, had no time to listen. The next day, thirty of us marched into the union hall. Sam jumped up from his desk, dusted off the chairs with his white handkerchief, and listened attentively. This reminds

me of the excellent advice embodied in the title of Frank and
Bea Lumpkin's book, *Always Bring a Crowd.*[12]

The push for a committee came mostly from recent addi-
tions to the orchestra. We immediately ran into problems with
the older musicians. There had been a committee in the past,
but it had been inoperative for several years. Since it had accomplished little, reviving it did not elicit much enthusiasm.
There was also resentment against us newcomers. Who did we
think we were, coming in and telling the old timers what ought
to be done?

A clique of first chair players felt they were the anointed
leaders of the orchestra and could represent it in any necessary
contacts with the conductor or the union.

William Zalken, the manager, and Max Steindel, the personnel manager, did everything they could to oppose a committee.
Even Golschmann got into the act. One day at rehearsal he
talked to the orchestra about how needless it was to form a
committee or to be confrontational about such things as pay
and working conditions.

"My friends," he said, "we are all musicians, we are artists.
We are not here for ze profit, we are here for ze art."

Newton astonished everybody by expressing his agreement
that we were indeed there for the sake of the music. He then
went on to say it was obvious that we were not there for money
or profit, since we were getting as little as $1,900 for a season's
work.

He added that since Golschmann was getting more than thirty
thousand per season it was unseemly of him to say that "we"
were not there for money. Newton suggested that if the conductor felt it necessary to interject himself into the dispute, he
should do so by backing the orchestra's demands.

Golschmann's face turned fiery red. He left the podium without replying and cancelled the remainder of the rehearsal.

The union was at first hostile to the idea of an orchestra
committee but finally gave us qualified permission. At the Local
2 Board of Directors meeting on February 25, 1952, the following action was taken:

"It was agreed that the Board shall not interpose any objec-
tion, at this time, if the personnel of the orchestra wishes to
elect an Orchestra Committee, on the condition and with the
understanding that said committee will not assume making any
decisions, and limiting its procedure and activities to informing

the M.M.B.A. Board of Directors concerning any situation or circumstances revealed to the committee by the personnel of the orchestra which should be considered or acted upon by the local."

Newton had decided not to return the following season, so he was willing to stick his neck out in the struggle for a committee, taking the lead in collecting signatures in favor. Before the end of that season, we had a majority. Newton so informed Max Steindel.

"Let me see the list," Max demanded.

Newton was not about to expose the signers to possible harassment, and said, "Oh, no. They stay right here in my pocket." We took them to the union and made the St. Louis Orchestra Committee official.

Russell always enjoys a good meal—especially on tour

Among the first orchestra committee chairpersons were the young, popular, and courageous Joe Gluck, Henry Loew, and Bob Maisel. The entire profession owes them a debt of gratitude.

Henry Loew also played an important part in getting the Committee. He had the prestige of the first chair of the bass section, the respect of the orchestra for his musicianship, and a personality that made him popular with his colleagues. No one could *not* like Henry—even orchestra managers.

Henry and Russell on tour

It was, of course, impossible to function within the restrictions imposed by the union board. Once the Committee was established it became more and more active as the voice of the orchestra, usually through the union but sometimes independently.

With less than half a year's work guaranteed, most of us were also guaranteed a period of unemployment every year. In the years when Virginia was not working, we had to borrow a few hundred dollars from family or friends before the fall Symphony season began, managing to pay it off by Christmas.

Some of the well-established local men did enough teaching to tide them over, but most of the single players left for New York or elsewhere to seek off-season work. Often they failed to return, accepting work in some other city with a greater prospect of permanence and family life.

Aron Teicher, a talented graphic artist as well as a violinist, portrayed our plight in a cartoon with several panels. First came a fiddle player in his formal concert clothes, holding his instrument at the end of the season. Then came several panels depicting him as a clerk, a welder, etc. Finally, in the fall, he was shown once more in white tie and tails with his fiddle under his chin. It was titled, "Vacation With Pay."

Even musicians in the larger orchestras, with somewhat longer seasons, had this problem. Two Philadelphia bass players, Fred Batchelder, my former roommate, and Ed Arian, with whom I had played in Central City, spent summers as "Good Humor" men, selling ice cream from carts on the street. A violist in our orchestra, Murray Schwartz, sold Fuller brushes between seasons. Henry Loew taught bass and also tuned pianos as a sideline.

Understandably, unemployment insurance was a major issue in the orchestra in the Fifties. Although a few musicians scorned it as "charity," most of us felt that it was desperately needed.

The Symphony Society, as a non-profit organization, was not required at that time to provide unemployment insurance and resisted adding this unwanted cost to the budget. In the negotiations for a new contract at the end of the 1958-59 season, the Orchestra Committee, with Ed Ormond as chair, made this a major demand, and it was won in 1960.

Another important victory of the Orchestra Committee was the establishment of a Dismissal Committee. Written into the contract, it bound the Society not to dismiss any member of the orchestra who had played two or more consecutive seasons without the approval of the Dismissal Committee. This Committee consisted of four members elected by the orchestra and four selected by the Symphony Society, which could include the conductor and the assistant conductor.

With the short season and the poor pay, some musicians became disgusted and left the symphonic field for positions in the music departments of universities. Others left music alto-gether.

Turnover was so great that thirty-one different bassists played in our eight-chair section in the decade of the Fifties. Three were older men who retired or died, but all the rest came and went, playing with us for a season or two and then going on to other orchestras or other jobs. By 1960, Henry and I, the new-comers a decade earlier, had become the old-timers, the only bassists who had been in the orchestra for a decade.

It was the same in the other sections. Of the eighty-eight members of the orchestra in 1960, only twenty-seven had been there in 1950.

When this problem was pointed out to Manager Zalken, his response was, "Musicians are like grasshoppers. They like to hop around."

Our struggle to improve pay and conditions was therefore also a struggle to develop a more stable orchestra, a struggle for better music. Yet it was not until the 1959-60 season that we finally were able to add two weeks to the previous twenty-three. Pay inched up by very small increments, not enough to make a substantial difference in the attractiveness of the job.

My own salary as assistant principal bass stayed a few dol-lars over minimum. In 1959-60 the minimum had reached $105 and my own pay $120 a week.

Although we had inadequate information about conditions in other orchestras, we knew enough to realize that these small improvements were not enough to keep us from dropping be-hind. We encountered some of the musicians from other sym-phonies when we were on tour and had friends in still other orchestras. The little information we had from these sources only reinforced our feeling that something must be done to es-tablish inter-orchestra communication.

How to do this was the subject of many discussions among orchestra members and particularly in the Committee, of which I was a member that year. Various proposals were made for surveying the symphonic scene, some quite elaborate.

Finally, Ed Ormond, Committee Chair, said, "It's got to be simple. A questionnaire to all orchestras as to their contracts and conditions and a return tabulation of the results."

While we were on tour we worked far into one night formu-lating the questionnaire. We got it copied and collected names of individuals in as many orchestras as we could. In some cases we sent it to a symphony hall addressed to "Orchestra Committee." We collated it with a covering letter on the bus between towns and sent it out.

Although we knew that what we were doing was important, in retrospect it can be said that its significance was immeasurable, not only to St. Louis, but to the whole symphonic profession. It was a major step toward what became, some years later, the International Conference of Symphony and Opera Musicians (ICSOM), part of the AFM.

Twenty orchestras reported on their conditions. Pay and length of season ranged from $70 a week for a twenty-week winter season and a four-week summer season in Denver to $157.50 a week in New York and Philadelphia for thirty-two week seasons. The Metropolitan Opera Orchestra members were getting $166.50 a week for thirty-one and a half weeks.

Eight of the orchestras were without Dismissal Committees and only five had the right to ratify their contracts. Only one (the New York Philharmonic) had a paid vacation. Only three

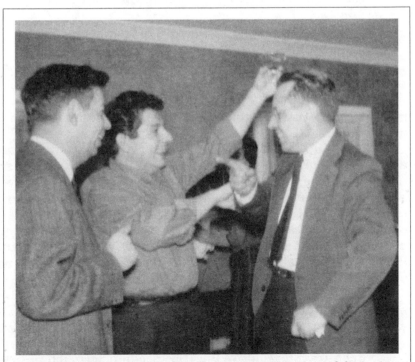

Ed Ormond, Al Genovese and Russell: a typically animated discussion

had any kind of health insurance paid by management. Seven had a pension plan. Fewer than half had unemployment insurance. The results of this survey are reproduced in the Appendix.

When we returned the compilation of answers to all those who had sent in information, we said, "the information compiled here has already been helpful to us in preparing contract proposals for next year and presenting our case to management. We hope it will be similarly helpful to other orchestras."

"It was gratifying," we continued, "to receive answers from other cities which were not only complete and interesting, but expressive of enthusiasm for the idea of inter-orchestra communication and further cooperation."

Here are some examples of the comments received:

- Excellent idea—Great need for clarification of working conditions and establishing liaison
- Your problems are our problems . . .
- The problems of the symphony musicians must be brought to the attention of members of Congress, public, etc.
- Perhaps it would be a good idea to have some sort of linkage among us all.
- I will discuss with the President of the Union the possibility of setting up a sort of convention for symphony players.

It seemed to us that the answers we received raised many new questions.

"How should musicians seek to better their present situation?" we asked when we circulated the tabulation of results. "Through our union, of course—certainly more regular, active participation in our locals, closer cooperation of orchestra personnel, orchestra committees and union officers is a basic necessity. But can each AFM Local solve each orchestra situation in isolation? Isn't a broader approach necessary? What about the proposal contained in more than one reply, that our International Union sponsor a symphony conference?"

Clearly our initiative had been timely. As Tom Hall put it in his history of ICSOM's first twenty-five years:

> ICSOM was the logical and inevitable outcome of a wave of militancy that swept through the ranks of orchestra musicians in the 1950's, characterized by anger and frustration growing from inadequate

wages, exploitive working conditions, and tenuous
job security long a part of orchestra careers . . . [13]

After several informal inter-orchestra meetings, representatives of fifteen orchestras (including St. Louis) met in Cleveland, September 6-8, 1962, and set up ICSOM. George Zazofsky
of the Boston Symphony was elected chairman. By 1968 membership had doubled to thirty orchestras, an annual tabulation
of pay and conditions similar to what we had initiated in St.
Louis was being produced and distributed, and a publication
was appearing several times a year with the appropriate title
Senza Sordino (Without Mute).

Most musicians never intended ICSOM to be a separate and
competing organization to the union, but in the early years,
especially, relations were strained. In 1969, ICSOM was granted
conference status within the Federation, which it still retains.
Annual conferences bring International AFM officers and presi-
dents of union locals representing symphony musicians together
with ICSOM officers and elected representatives of all member
orchestras, which numbered fifty by the year 2000.

ICSOM has had a major effect in improving the pay and conditions of musicians in symphony and opera. That history, however, is beyond the scope of this memoir. While ICSOM was
getting under way, there was drama enough on the St. Louis
stage.

ORCHESTRA vs. CONDUCTOR

The 1957-58 season was Golschmann's twenty-seventh and last. Even during that season, he conducted only ten of the twenty pairs of subscription concerts. Guest conductors led the others as the Society looked for a replacement.

Who that successor would be was of vital interest to all of us. There is a world of difference between making music with a creative, inspiring leader and trying to make music in spite of a dull and limited leader. There is also a world of difference between working for a conductor who sees musicians as people who are co-workers and one who sees them as things, mere pieces of his instrument.

As the episodes with Golschmann show, the conductor, although a member of the union, is much more likely to be an ally of the management than of the players. In the hands of the new conductor would be the power to hire and fire, only slightly modified by the establishment of a Dismissal Committee.

After the first of four concerts with Georg Solti conducting all the Beethoven Symphonies, the word began to get around, and each succeeding concert drew a larger audience. He did not become the permanent conductor in St. Louis, however. Perhaps the Society was unwilling to meet his conditions. He wanted the freedom to continue conducting in Europe, and perhaps asked for more than the Society was willing to pay.

In any case, an opportunity to get a truly great conductor was missed. Solti went to Los Angeles, and subsequently to Chicago. Eduoard Van Remoortel, a little-known young Belgian conductor, was hired instead. One of his attractions, from the Society's point of view, was that he came from an influential European banking family, and apparently exuded charm in his social relations.

The orchestra was not charmed. As his first season progressed, his musical limitations became more and more obvious. He had a narrow repertoire, was inflexible in rehearsals and superficial in interpretation. Some of his procedures were downright stupid. He insisted that the first violins be seated in an exact row, one stand directly behind the other in military precision. This made it difficult for a short person behind a tall person to see the conductor.

At the end of his first season, Thomas Sherman, the *Post-Dispatch* critic, summed him up in a phrase: "unimaginative competence."

In the spring of his first season, unsettling rumors circulated that he planned to replace a third of the orchestra in each of three successive seasons, giving him a young orchestra entirely chosen by him. When challenged by the Orchestra Committee about the rumors, he flatly denied that he had any such intention.

According to *Symphony and Song*, the history of the St. Louis Symphony's first hundred years, the rumor underestimated his intention. He at first planned to fire half the orchestra: 42 of the 85 musicians, but "narrowed it down," probably at the advice of the Society's leaders.[14]

The reality, presented to the Orchestra Committee by the conductor just before a scheduled tour, proved to be a list of seventeen, still a shockingly high number. The Committee announced that seventeen were threatened with firing but did not release the names on the list. Everyone felt threatened, knowing that he or she might be on the list. Even if not, no one could be secure in subsequent seasons if the conductor could get away with wholesale dismissals. Outrage surged through the orchestra. The Committee, then chaired by George Hussey (English horn, later first oboe) was besieged by demands to do something.

An orchestra meeting was called just prior to the final concert before the tour. This was a most unusual meeting with all of us dressed for work in white tie and tails or long black gowns, some with instruments in hand. The audience was assembling in the auditorium. The conductor and the guest soloist, Marian Anderson, were ready in their dressing rooms.

The audience waited in increasing wonder for the musicians to appear on the stage and begin tuning up. For Virginia and the few others "in the know," the suspense grew by the minute. Just by chance, Virginia ran into music critic Sherman and his wife and told them what was going on. Sherman asked Manager William Zalken about it and was told it was "just a little matter of musician temperament."

Meanwhile, the 85 "temperamental" musicians were debating, not whether to demonstrate their outrage, but how. Finally, we decided to postpone our protest action to the following morning's pre-tour rehearsal. Clarinetist Earl Bates, one of the Committee members, went to Ms. Anderson's dressing room to apologize for the delay and explain to her that we had decided to play the concert in deference to her. The orchestra played well, with obvious excitement.

Everyone reported for duty that next morning but when the conductor walked on to the stage and raised his baton, not a bow was lifted, not a horn came up to lips. That was a tense moment. The refusal to respond to the conductor's baton is so contrary to the habits of years of performing that it took considerable self-discipline.

Hussey informed Van Remoortel that the orchestra had decided not to perform for him because of his proposed firings. One interested listener to the controversy was a reporter from the *St. Louis Post-Dispatch.* He had been tipped off by Sherman, always sympathetic to the musicians and not at all convinced that this was a mere tempest in a temperamental teapot.

The *Post-Dispatch* reported Van Remoortel's response to Hussey: "'This is not the right time or the right place to discuss the matter. I will be glad to take up the question in detail at the appropriate time. For now, we have a concert and a tour.'"

The newspaper report continued:

> The 85 orchestra members received his remarks in silence. "Is this a strike?" he asked.
>
> Henry Loew, bass player and member of the orchestra committee, replied: "This is not a strike. We will fulfill our contract. We are ready to play, but we will not play for you until you settle this matter."[15]

The conductor left the stage and the Committee—Hussey, Loew, Bates, and Ormond—met with him. He agreed to submit the dismissals to the Dismissal Committee as called for by the contract, and the musicians agreed to rehearse.

The problem simmered throughout the tour. The Committee was concerned about maintaining the unity of the orchestra and the backing of the union until the tour was over and the Dismissal Committee could meet.

The orchestra knew seventeen musicians were targeted, but the conductor could not now give them notice. The Committee kept the list secret in order to keep the unity strong.

One cellist who feared he was on the list, said to Henry Loew, "Henry, I have to know if I'm on the list. My wife is pregnant. We'll be in real trouble if I get fired."

"All right," Henry said. "You're on the list. How do you feel?"

"Terrible."

Then Henry said, "No, you're not on the list. How do you feel now?"

"I still feel terrible."

When we returned from tour, auditions were held before the Dismissal Committee, composed of both players and management representatives. Two older men on the list decided to retire and did not audition. The Dismissal Committee took eight people off the list. Van Rcmoortel agreed that their jobs were secure for both the coming season and the one to follow. Of the seven who had to leave, several had been in the orchestra only one season. They were considered to be on trial, and the Dismissal Committee had no jurisdiction over their jobs.

In spite of saving eight musicians, the orchestra lost a total of eighteen. The other eleven were not people Van Remoortel would have chosen. First oboe Alfred Genovese and assistant principal viola Ed Ormond, for example, went to Cleveland where the season was longer, the pay better and the musical direction from George Szell vastly superior. They were a real loss to the orchestra.

Although rclations bctwccn conductor and orchestra were better the second year, and Van Remoortel had apparently learned a lesson when it came to firing, we still lost twenty people at the end of that season. Among them were violinists Joan and Bert Siegel, who joined the Pittsburgh Orchestra.

Harpist Graziella Pampari and her husband, Pasquale DeConto, retired after 37 years in the orchestra. DeConto was bitter that after all those years, there was no pension for either. He told a colleague that the head of the Symphony Society had offered him a single payment of $500, which he returned, saying it was not a pension, it was an insult.

During Van Remoortel's third season we went on tour through the south. Conflict surfaced again, this time on a question of musical quality. The leadership from the podium was so inadequate and the conductor's behavior so unprofessional that the Committee felt something had to be done.

We later characterized the concert in Columbia, Mississippi, by saying that "the music was not well performed, the soloist not adequately supported, the orchestra's reputation jeopardized and the audience shortchanged."

Chairman Jim Emde (tuba) and two other members of the Committee, bassists Robert Maisel and myself, went to Van Remoortel's hotel room in Rome, Georgia, the next day to discuss the problem.

He refused to acknowledge either that there was anything wrong or that the Committee had any business speaking to him about it.

When Maisel suggested that he might have had too much to drink before the concert—which was all too obvious—he jumped to his feet and shouted, "Out! Out! Out!" The length of the conference was three minutes.

We got through the remaining 20 concerts on tour somehow. None was quite as bad as the Columbia concert.

After the season was over and the out-of-town musicians had left, Van Remoortel filed charges with the Union accusing Emde, Maisel and me of insulting him and treating him unfairly. Of course we countercharged.

Contracts were distributed to the other musicians, but not to us. Twenty musicians came to a meeting in our support, and later a committee was formed to give us help, including financial assistance.

THREE IN SYMPHONY FINED $10 BY UNION

Three St. Louis' Symphony Orchestra musicians who were charged with violating the constitution of Local 2 of the American Federation of Musicians have been found guilty and fined $10 each, Kenneth J. Farmer, president of the local, said today.

At the same time, Farmer reported, the local's board of directors "will insist that the three men's contracts with the Symphony Orchestra be renewed next season."

The three—James Emde, Robert Maisel and Russell Brodine—had been accused by Symphony conductor Edouard Van Remoortel of violating the local's constitution by not acting in good faith and not dealing fairly with him.

The charge grew out of a visit the three men made to Van Remoortel in his hotel room in Rome, Ga., last March 2, when the orchestra was on a concert tour of the South. They protested to him against his conduct Feb. 28 at a concert in Columbus, Miss.

A dispute ensued and Van Remoortel ordered the three from his room. Later he filed charges against them with the local. The three musicians filed notice of plans to make a counter-charge against Van Remoortel, but to date have not done so, Farmer reported.

The three men have been informed of their right to appeal the finding to the union's national executive board, Farmer said. They have not indicated yet whether they will, he said. The investigation of the charges was conducted by the local's board of directors.

The final outcome was that the union backed up the Orchestra's demand that we get our contract but we were found guilty of some of the charges by the Local Union Board, the verdict sustained on appeal by the International. We got a tap on the wrist—a ten-dollar fine.

Van Remoortel's contract was not renewed. He conducted only seven concerts the following season and I believe never again conducted in the United States. Rumor had it that he returned to Europe and became an auto salesman.

I will say that at one point I did feel some compassion for Eduoard Van Remoortel. His parents visited from Belgium and attended a concert at the Chase Hotel. The conductor's make-shift dressing room was anything but private. The applause ended at intermission, and he left the podium. I carefully laid my fiddle down and walked down past the dressing room in search of fresh air. I was by accident right behind his parents. I was not eavesdropping, but I couldn't help but hear his mother say in a commanding voice, "Son, can't you do anything right?" What an unfortunate upbringing little Eduoard must have had amongst the wealthy upper crust of Europe!

The 1962-63 season brought us a series of guest conductors, obviously auditioning for the position of permanent conductor. With the disaster of 1958 in mind, the Orchestra was deeply concerned about the choice.

About two-thirds of the way through the season, the musicians decided to make their opinions known. A poll was taken on the eight conductors under consideration and the results communicated to the Union and the Society. One conductor, reputed to be highly regarded by the Society, was at the bottom of almost every list. His subsequent career bore out this judgment.

When another guest conductor had appeared, the Society requested that the Orchestra take another poll, so the final candidate could be included. Three conductors got high ratings from the players.

The one receiving the highest rating in both polls, Eleazar de Carvalho, was hired. He was one of the few conductors whom I really respected. He was not only from Brazil but was truly Braziliano. In conducting South American music, he could almost make both the musicians and audiences want to tango. He remained for five years, and his tenure was marked by the addition to our programs of many modern works. One result of his emphasis on very modern difficult scores was that the orchestra became very versatile. But he also did the classics with great feeling and excitement. I looked forward to his rehearsals, and especially to the concerts with anticipation. Never a dull moment.

Having in his youth been in the Brazil navy band playing tuba, he certainly came from a culture vastly different from mine and had an almost military respect for authority. For one or two years during his tenure, I was Committee chair. He addressed me as "El Capitan." At first I thought it was with tongue in cheek. Not so. In Committee conferences also he deferred to the wisdom of the Orchestra in a thoughtful and respectful manner, something very unusual in a conductor.

TOWARD EQUALITY

For many years, the St. Louis Symphony was all male and all white except the bass clarinetist, who was Mexican. *Symphony and Song* begins the story of the orchestra's first hundred years with a picture of the city in the late 19th century as "a blend of nationalities . . . the large German population. . . the Irish . . . the French . . . smaller contingents from Russia and various Central European countries" which "gave St. Louis . . . a colorful personality."[16] Only St. Louisans of European heritage are mentioned, and in regard to music, the German choral societies indeed gave birth to the Symphony.

But there was another musical culture growing in the city, and people of African heritage were an important part of the city's "colorful personality." St. Louis is known for its role in the early history of jazz. The musical life of the city in 1907 is described in *Symphony and Song* without a word about either the jazz tradition or that of the choral religious music of the black churches.

Unionism, like the Symphony, began among German-Americans. An Aschenbroedel Club broadened to become the Musical Mutual Protective Union. As noted earlier, when the American Federation of Musicians, AFL was formed in 1896, the St. Louis union was one of the founding groups, becoming Local 2. The first president of the Federation was a St. Louis man, George Miller.[17]

Not long after (the exact date is uncertain), African-American musicians in St. Louis organized their own union, which joined the Federation as Local 44. In 1932, it became subsidiary to Local 2. Opposition to this subsidiary status grew in St. Louis and in the eleven other cities where it existed and in 1944 all gained or regained their autonomy. The St. Louis union became Local 197.[18]

Some of the locals in northern cities were always integrated, but in 1944 there were still 50 African-American locals in the Federation.

There were no African-American musicians in the St. Louis
Symphony and none of the great singers such as Roland Hayes
and Paul Robeson soloed with the orchestra. Finally, after World
War II and after the death of the most obstinate bigot on the
Symphony Board, that bar was dropped. Marian Anderson,
Dorothy Maynard and other African-American singers performed
with us, making an outstanding addition to our musical life.
But we still had an all-white orchestra.

Our Los Angeles friend's prediction that we would find St.
Louis to be "a northern city with a southern exposure" proved
to be only too true.

Max Steindel, the personnel manager, who also hired musicians for outside jobs, was adamant in his determination to
maintain segregation. I also heard racist remarks all too often
from other musicians. I never allowed one of these remarks to
go unanswered. To do so is to encourage their repetition. To
challenge them is to help make them less acceptable.

Of course, I got the old, worn out racist/sexist response,
"You wouldn't want your daughter to marry one."

My answer to this 6'4" fiddle player was, "Well, there is one
kind of person I would prefer that she never marry."

"Yeah, who?" He replied with a satisfied smirk.

"A bigot."

The first time I challenged Max, one of my friends told me he
would never hire me again for an outside job. Not so. He continued to hire me, but that was small consolation, since all his
jobs remained lily-white.

Two Filipino-Americans, violinist Leonard Austria and harpist Maria Muribus, and one Japanese-American, Teruko Akagi,
were hired for the symphony in the Fifties, but still no African-
Americans. This made others beside myself increasingly uncomfortable.

Several of us had informal meetings with members and officers of Local 197 about breaking down the barriers, and we
began to seek qualified African-American musicians who would
be willing to audition.

Finding them was not easy, because it was difficult for black
students to get classical training and not many were willing to
embark on it if they could get it, since they were aware that
opportunities for them in the field were almost non-existent.

With the help of Nat Hentoff, who was at that time crusad-
ing for equal opportunities in music in the pages of *Downbeat*,

we did get some African-American musicians to audition for St. Louis when auditions were held in New York in the late 'sixties. Although none were hired at that time, it made a tiny crack in a wall that had been in place for many years. One bass player who auditioned was qualified and would have been welcomed in the bass section. We were prepared to press for his hiring, but he had an offer from a jazz group on tour that was so much better financially that he could not afford to accept the Symphony job.

A letter was circulated through the orchestra asking for an end to discrimination in hiring, to be sent to the Symphony Society and the Local 2 Executive Board. Many signed it, but no action followed.

In 1964 several of my colleagues, Henry Loew, Jerome Rosen, and Alexander Lydzinski, together with William Schatzkamer of the Washington University music faculty, started the Gateway Festival Orchestra, which is still in existence.

Also associated with the project were community leaders Kenneth Billups, Lily Kaufman, and Martin Lanznar. The purpose was to provide free concerts to be performed by 50 musicians playing great music from the symphonic repertoire at the riverfront near the new Gateway Arch. George Smith, president of Local 197 was cooperative, and an appeal to Local 2 also brought sufficient funds to cover three concerts. During its first season, eleven of its fifty members were from Local 197.[19]

The same year the Gateway started, a growing trend for integration in the American Federation of Musicians became official policy. A Civil Rights Department was established with former president Petrillo as chair. Its job was to complete "the orderly merger of its remaining dual locals serving single jurisdictions." [20]

There was reluctance in Local 2 based on racism, and reluctance in 197 based on fear of again losing their autonomy. With Petrillo's guidance, however, the leaders of the two Locals worked out a merger agreement.

At last, in 1968, African-American musicians joined the Symphony. Like the union's integration of its locals, this came as a result of the Civil Rights movement.

When Dr. Martin Luther King, Jr. was assassinated, the sorrow and anger that swept the country was felt by musicians as well. The Orchestra Committee proposed a memorial concert for King. Agreement was enthusiastic. Participation was voluntary but nearly complete. At the invitation of the Committee, several musicians from the Gateway Orchestra joined us for the concert, including Charlene Clark.

Charlene was a student of Jerry Rosen's and one of the early members of the Gateway. She had auditioned for the St. Louis orchestra but had been turned down.

Her demonstrated ability in the memorial concert led to the offer of a contract for the following season. That broke the ice, and that same season another African-American violinist, Joe Striplin from Detroit, auditioned and was hired. Joe later achieved his childhood dream of playing in the Detroit Symphony, but Charlene remained in the St. Louis Symphony. The contingent of Japanese-Americans has grown, but to this day there are very few African-American orchestra members.

Also missing from the pages of *Symphony and Song* is the musical career of one of the outstanding musical educators in the city, the late Kenneth Billups, a distinguished African-American musician. He has already been mentioned in connection with the Gateway Orchestra. He was for many years music director at Sumner High School and the teacher of several singers who went on to distinguished opera careers, Grace Bumbry being the best known. He also conducted a fine adult chorus, which occasionally sang with us. Billups was belatedly added to the Symphony Board in 1971.

An unexpected accolade from the management in recognition of my reputation as a champion of racial equality was that when Leonard Austria was hired, and subsequently Joe Striplin, each was assigned to me as a locker-mate in town and a roommate on tour.

The barrier against women performers, like that against African-Americans, was slow to break down. The excuse was that there were no dressing rooms for women. Except for the harpist, there had been no woman in the orchestra until the 1943-44 season, when the wartime shortage of available men opened the way for women and five were hired. By 1950 there were nine women in the orchestra, and when I left in 1973, there were twenty-four.

Hiring was only the first step, however. The women had other manifestations of sexism to contend with. They took action, individually or collectively in their own behalf and sometimes had the support of the Orchestra Committee or the entire orchestra.

Sexism was not absent among the male musicians. When husband and wife were both in the orchestra, the husband—regardless of the relative skill and talent of himself and his wife—sometimes insisted that she not be advanced ahead of him in the section.

I once told such a man that I had a medical researcher friend who had come up with a new drug that would be just the thing for him. That got his attention and I told him, "You can administer it to your wife. It's a 'stupid' pill."

When Manager Zalken presented the 1962-63 contracts to the musicians, there was one clause in the women's contracts that had not been agreed to by either the Orchestra Committee or the Union:

> The parties hereto mutually acknowledge that concerts by the orchestra are both artistic and aesthetic performances, and recognize that any physical or other condition which can result in audience distraction or cause concern for other than musical matters will necessarily affect these performances. It is understood and agreed by both parties that if the undersigned musician is or becomes pregnant at anytime during the term of the 1962-63 season and such pregnancy is visually apparent or causes interference with the ability of the party of the second part to render proper services, then and in any such event this contract may be terminated by either party and such termination shall become effective immediately upon the giving of such notice.

I read that clause over three times; each time it sounded more disgusting. The next day we had an orchestra meeting on the stage after rehearsal. I pulled the contract out of my pocket and reminded my colleagues that this piece of paper was always with us—figuratively speaking—when we went to the supermarket, when we went to buy a car, (slapping my hand with the contract with each example), when we went house-hunting and so on and on.

"But I'll be goddamned," I said, "if it's such a good contract that anyone should have to take it to bed with them."

The stage rocked with laughter and jeers. Humor triumphed. The clause quietly disappeared from the women's contracts.

But smashing an evil is not the same as winning a good, although this event did strengthen the coalition between men and women in the orchestra. I knew I was only clearing away the brush for subsequent fights for maternity benefits. Those fights were subsequently won. In the 1991-94 agreement, the clause read in part as follows:

> Maternity leave shall be granted by the Society with no loss of tenure or position, with or without pay as hereinafter provided, the beginning and end of such maternity leave to be decided upon by the Musician and her physician. For Musicians with at least one (1) year of service, the Society shall grant sick leave or maternity leave with pay for up to a total of twenty-six (26) weeks in any season.

Side by side with these struggles and those for such basic questions as improvements in pay and length of season, we had a struggle over more intangible things that had to do with being treated with the dignity we deserved as artists and as human beings, actually another aspect of the struggle for equality.

Sometimes it was a trivial matter such as the way the paychecks were handed out. The librarian was responsible, and one payday he took out his irritation on us by laying the checks out on the floor so that we would have to stoop down to pick them up. We wouldn't accept them until they were handed to us.

A much more serious matter surfaced when we gathered for rehearsal one morning during the 1958-59 season. Vincent Grimaldi, one of the bass players, was absent. Grimaldi had been a member of the section for many years, at one time its principal. He seldom missed a service. However, he was not in perfect health, and we assumed that a minor illness was keeping him out.

When he failed to report for work the next day, we asked Max Steindel what the trouble was.

"He better show up or he lose his goddamn job," was the answer.

On the third day of Grimaldi's absence, Henry Loew and I called but could get no answer. After rehearsal we went to the rooming house where he lived alone. We found him sitting in a chair, dead. He had lived gently. He died gently.

There was to be a concert the next evening. We felt that Grimaldi's years of service and his lonely passing should not go unnoticed. We asked that the funeral march from Beethoven's Third Symphony, already on the program, be dedicated to his memory. Manager Zalken refused the request.

While we played the concert, the refusal rankled. Rosemary Goldsmith was particularly outraged. She was a very fine violist, totally dedicated to good music. Rosemary was always willing to see another person's point of view and was slow to complain.

Several of us, including Rosemary, went out for an after-concert snack in an Italian restaurant. She said bitterly that this was just too much and could not be allowed to pass without protest. We composed a letter on the spot and all signed it. The next day, Rosemary took it around the orchestra and gathered additional signatures.

The letter began with this quotation from Shakespeare's *Julius Caesar:*

When beggars die there are no comets seen;

The heavens themselves blaze forth the death of princes

It then pointed out that when a member of the Symphony Association died, he was memorialized at a concert, as we had wanted to do for Grimaldi, but "Vincent had no money, he could only give music."

It appeared in the *Post-Dispatch* a few days later, with the notation that it was "signed by Rosemary Goldsmith and twenty other members of the St. Louis Symphony." Zalken was infuriated, but at the next concert a number was dedicated to Grimaldi's memory.

That was not the end of the episode, however. When the first chair in the viola section was open at the end of that season, Rosemary applied for the position. There could be no question about her qualifications, but she was denied the promotion. Her musicianship was not criticized, but the conductor, Van Remoortel, asked her, "Aren't you one of those people who write letters?"

A few years later, when the second chair was again open, Rosemary was moved up, but by this time she was disaffected, looked for a position in another orchestra, and we soon lost her to Cleveland.

From our early days in St. Louis, Rosemary and George Goldsmith were among our close friends, and we enjoyed many parties and celebrations together. George had piercing questions and equally piercing observations on life, ecology and the arts. Through her intensity in the orchestra, Rosemary showed her very great devotion to her art. Less inclined than George to be vocal in opinions on politics, she was a lover of nature. She and I were the two members on tours who most often took nature hikes.

Virginia and I always treasured our relationship with Rosemary and George. Neither ever spoke much of their life in Nazi Germany, but their story has been told by their son, Martin Goldsmith, in *The Inextinguishable Symphony.*[21]

Violist Rosemary Goldsmith and Russell
during a tour to Florida

VARIATIONS ON THE WORK THEME

The FBI had cost me at least one job. During the Fifties we never knew when it might get me fired from the St. Louis Symphony. I began to think about an auxiliary trade that might help tide us over between seasons, and in case I got fired, could keep us going. I chose stringed instrument repair, in part because it would keep me close to music and musicians and because I like working with wood.

The best stringed instruments were all old, and the older they got the better they sounded, but often they were in need of repair. Curtis had a collection of fine instruments, so as a student I had played on nothing but the best. Just before leaving the east, I bought a Mittenwald bass, made in Austria. This was the instrument with the low notes I played for Stokowski in the Hollywood Bowl. I had begun to work on this bass myself when it needed re-pair.

Now I found an old Hungarian fiddle-maker who was willing to take me on as an apprentice—a "learnpoop" he called me. In exchange for my help in his shop, he taught me the trade.

Soon I was working on other bass fiddles, on guitars, and then on the stringed instruments from a high school music department. Instrument repair never had to become

Repairing the top of a dismantled bass

a full-time occupation, but it did supplement my symphony income, and I enjoyed the work. What I liked least was rehairing bows. What I liked best was making my own bow.

I worked on basses more than on any other instruments and later bought another bass for myself. It was an old Italian instrument made by Michaelangelo Nardelli. I sold the Mittenwald to Joe Kleeman when he joined the Symphony. Joe Kleeman is a no-non-

Making his own bass bow

sense, dependable person, who served on the Orchestra Committee and later became assistant personnel manager of the orchestra.

My symphony pay was also augmented by other music work. Two summer jobs were open to those who had established their regular membership in Local 2: the Municipal Opera, a twelve-week season of light opera and musicals in Forest Park, and

the Little Symphony, a six-week chamber orchestra season in the quadrangle at Washington University.

I began playing the Little Symphony in the summer of 1951, and in 1953 played both jobs, getting a substitute at "Muni Opera" when there was a conflict. I disliked the Muni job, which was neither truly municipal nor was it opera. It required sawing away in the St. Louis heat for more than eighty consecutive nights plus daytime rehearsals. This schedule made it difficult for us to do anything recreational as a family in the summer.

An open drain was just behind the bass section, making the orchestra pit and especially our area unpleasantly smelly. We lowered a bottle into the drain and pulled up a sample of the water, which we took to a lab for testing. We then had proof that the water was contaminated, but that wasn't enough for the personnel manager. He played in the viola section, which was next to ours, but claimed that he couldn't smell anything.

One of the bass players slipped in quietly before a concert on one hot and humid night and smeared Limburger cheese under the personnel manager's chair. This time outrage over the dreadful odor was carried to higher authorities. We finally got something done about our own special air pollution. Underhanded? Well, maybe!

The Little Symphony season was shorter and paid less per week than Muni Opera, but the music was more interesting. Being the only bass, I found it much more challenging work.

The Muni management was unwilling to allow me to provide substitutes for the following season, so I had to choose between the two. If I chose the Little Symphony it would mean a considerable loss in pay. However, we now had two paychecks in the family. Virginia was working in the regional office of the International Ladies Garment Workers' Union. We agreed that the better music and a little more family life were worth the difference. I accepted the Little Symphony and rejected the Muni Opera.

Occasionally between symphony seasons, I had an opportunity to take a short tour with a chamber orchestra. This gave me some of my most memorable musical experiences. Although chamber music—quartets, quintets, etc.—has few compositions with bass parts, the chamber orchestra of ten to twenty musicians (usually with a single bass), has a wealth of fine music. Much of it was composed prior to the days of the large symphony. We played music by Bach, Vivaldi, Mozart and others.

One of these off-season tours was with a group led by the violinist Henry Temianka. I had once played the *Trout* with him in Hollywood at a party at the home of screenwriter Harry Kurnitz. The musicians were playing as a kind of "thank you" for the help Kurnitz had given to musicians working in the film industry.

Temianka's tour group was excellent. It was a pleasure to play with him and the other musicians on works outside the symphony repertoire.

Another chamber orchestra was "Music for Tonight" led by Al Tipton, principal flute in the St. Louis Symphony. Next to me in that group was Leslie Parnas, a great cellist who has since become famous. The two of us could engage in musical subtleties not possible in symphonic work.

Both these chamber groups produced very sensitive music, making these experiences a real pleasure. The audiences, sometimes in places that seldom had an opportunity to hear live classical music, responded enthusiastically.

Being a member of a great 90-100 piece symphony orchestra, playing at maximum volume to an audience of a thousand or more listeners is a superlative experience. Performing in a small group to a smaller audience is intimate and inspiring beyond words.

Being the only bass in these groups, as in the Little Symphony, was a much greater responsibility than being a member of a section of eight or more. When the music went well, it was also individually rewarding. The gratification was probably somewhat similar to what a soloist enjoys—a feeling that seldom comes the way of a bass player.

Less enjoyable was my tour with a symphonette. It seemed even longer than its eight weeks. The conductor (who shall remain nameless here) laid down the law like a sergeant.

"Tomorrow morning the bus leaves on time," he decreed one evening, after a few days when we had waited ten or fifteen minutes for stragglers. "No matter who is late!"

Guess who was late. We took a vote on whether to wait for him or to proceed according to his dictates. We knew there was public transportation available, so the vote was unanimous. We drove off minus our esteemed conductor.

Early in the tour I had a disagreement with the conductor about some small matter. A few days later the personnel manager called me over and said, "He likes your playing. You can be his bass man on future tours. He'll forget about what you said to him last week. Now tell me, what are the guys saying about him?"

That was the prime insult of my whole professional career. No one else before or since ever imagined that I could be turned into a stool pigeon.

My roommate, Murray Schwartz, a talented violist, also had his difficulties with this particular conductor. He was handed a discharge in Spokane giving him two weeks notice.

At our room in the Pennington Hotel, Murray and I threw a little party for the musicians and our bus driver. Conn Armour, the driver, a Native American, was well liked by us all and was as much a part of the group as if he played an instrument.

We discussed the firing and agreed to stick by Murray. If he went, we would all go. We drew up a resignation to be effective just prior to our Chicago concert, the most important of the tour. All signed it. Conn expressed his solidarity by volunteering to present the resignation.

All of us, including Murray, completed the tour.

One enjoyable job for a short time in each of two summers was the Fish Creek Music Festival. Fish Creek is in Door County, Wisconsin, the beautiful peninsula that separates Green Bay from Lake Michigan. Sandy beaches on one side of the peninsula and rocky shores on the other provided many great places for swimming and picnicking. The family accompanied me, so it was a pleasant vacation for all of us.

Ed Ormond also played that job, so our two families vacationed together. What added to the enjoyment was renewing old friendships. My former Curtis roommate, Fred Batchelder, was the leader in the bass section. George and Sylvia Martin, with whom I had lived during my student years, were there with their youngest son, now a cellist.

Every St. Louis Symphony season included a tour, usually of about three weeks. The eastern tour with a Carnegie Hall concert during my first season was unusual. We more frequently toured the Midwest and upper south, a monotonous grind of bus travel and one-night stands.

I mentioned earlier that these conditions sometimes helped to develop militancy and solidarity, but this was by no means always the case. Any group of 80 or 90 people, musicians included, contains some who turn irritations over poor accommodations, stressful scheduling and so on into irritation with one another or into general unpleasantness for everybody.

We traveled in three buses. The "A" bus was the prestige bus. The conductor was in that bus when he traveled with the orchestra, as he usually did, also the assistant conductor, the personnel manager and those first chair players and others who gravitated toward prestige.

The "B" bus was the hurry-up bus. Those most interested in covering the miles as fast as possible and getting to our destination first chose "B". (Maybe they had *schpilkes in tokas*.)

My choice was always the "C" bus. It was variously known as "the collective farm" or "the garbage department." It attracted those who were oriented toward collective action for our betterment, and/or collective fun to make the tour more bearable.

The "B" bus once dropped behind the other two buses, which was very unusual. The weather was bad and roads were slick. The bus slid and hit a concrete abutment. No one was killed, but the injuries that resulted ended more than one performing career. Insurance adjusters got there quickly and dangled small checks in front of the injured. Those who accepted had no further claim. Some were more prudent and were able to get more justice.

One problem that sometimes arose on tour was the unauthorized recording of a concert. When we protested, it might be claimed that it was "for personal use only." Perhaps, but the union had to put up a constant struggle to get the musicians paid for their work, including when it was recorded, so union rules were strict on this matter.

On one occasion, we followed wires running from the stage into a backstage room with a locked door. I knocked on the door, which opened, and a very white face looked out. That man knew he was breaking the rules, probably with the intention of selling a few black market records. We saw to it that he removed his wire.

On a lighter and happier note, during the period when the now-famous St. Louis Arch was being constructed, we were on tour in Wisconsin. There was a beautiful, fresh snow in front of our motel, perfect material for a 10-foot replica of the Arch. We also erected an imposing snow-woman. The snow sculptures got nationwide photo-media coverage.

On one of our southern tours we arrived in Galveston, Texas, with a few hours to spare before our first concert. Several of us "C" bus characters rented a pleasure craft for a spin in the bay. It was a delightful change from the long hours of confinement on the bus. Everything was fine until we were far from shore. Then the motor conked out, and we were adrift.

We waved to passing boats to get help but people merely waved back in a friendly way. Finally, Murray Schwartz climbed on top of the cabin and waved his white shirt as a signal of distress. Henry Loew revived his wartime Signal Corps knowledge of Morse code. Piercingly, repeatedly, he whistled "S-O-S!"

At last, the Coast Guard arrived and towed us in, just in time for the concert. We had no time to change into our concert clothes, but hurried on to the stage in informal dress. Our adventure put the St. Louis Orchestra in the national news once more.

Murray Schwartz (center) signaling for help in Galveston Harbor

While the orchestra was away on one tour, Virginia and some of the other wives who remained behind decided to welcome us back with a dinner and a skit. The performance was a take-off on touring. The captains of the three buses were impersonated. A "concert" had Grace Hussey conducting. The "orchestra" descended on a restaurant where Mildred Loew as the waitress sang, "If I'd known you were coming, I'd have baked a cake."

The theme song (written by Virginia) was sung to the tune of Irving Berlin's "I Joined the Navy to See the World":

We joined the Symphony to see the world,
And what do we see? Just Kankakee.
We joined the symphony to see the world,
But where do we go? We go to St. Joe.
We hear that the Philly's going to Europe
And that the Boston's getting a tour up
Seems it will take them into both London and Paree.
They joined a Symphony, to see the world,
But where do we play? In I-o-way,
Dubuque and Des Monies and all the scenic spots along
the way. (and so on)

Tours generally took place in the spring, just prior to contract negotiations for the following season. They played a special role in preparing for those negotiations.

On tour there is endless talking on the buses, in the hotels and restaurants, at after-concert parties. Developing unity around our current move toward improving conditions often began in the "C" bus and spread through the orchestra. This

Wood carvings, from a photo feature in the St. Louis Post-Dispatch
Russell is holding a carving he made of Cynthia reading.

was especially true on the 1965 tour. We were working under a two-year contract that no one liked. Inadequate negotiations for this contract in 1963 had been extended and difficult. We had asked for a 32-week season (up from 25) and a substantial pay increase. The Society's final offer was for 27 weeks the first year and 30 the second with only a $5 raise in the minimum in each of the two years.

The orchestra had rejected this offer, 42-13, but the Society refused to budge. Orchestra Committee and union had tried hard through the summer. As the time for the opening concert approached, the Society threatened to cancel the season unless we accepted their offer. It was accept or strike, and it was not clear that the orchestra as a whole was ready to strike. The contract was accepted under protest.

Relations with the Society did not improve during the life of that contract. One Board member, in a Management/Committee meeting, complained that the musicians were "immature" and did not appreciate what was being done for them by the Board members who donated their services.

We had our demands for the next contract worked out by January of 1965, but at tour time there had been no response from management. Much of our talk during that tour was purposeful—building unity behind those demands.

STRIKE!

During our 1964-65 season, the minimum in the Symphony, establishing the salary for eighty per cent of the orchestra, was only $130 a week, $3,900 for the 30-week season. We were not only far behind the "big five"—New York, Philadelphia, Boston, Chicago, and Cleveland—but even behind Rochester, Cincinnati, and other cities of comparable size.

Contact with representatives of other orchestras through ICSOM was keeping St. Louis musicians abreast of what was happening elsewhere. Salaries were reaching and passing $200 a week and seasons were moving toward—in some cases achieving—a full 52-week season.

We, too, were determined to move our orchestra in the direction of year-round employment and a ten thousand dollar annual salary. In the mid-sixties that would have been reasonable, though not affluent.

We had taken one step with that two-year contract in 1963, but progress at the rate of a few weeks a year would not get us a 52-week season for about ten years. Meanwhile our salary would continue at poverty level. Our experience in 1963 showed that it would take a hard struggle with management to maintain even that pace.

The Society's business manager worked for the Symphony only part time, which made him incapable of raising the funds required by a first-class orchestra. He spent half his time bringing other musical attractions to the city; a longer season would put the symphony in competition with his other interests.

We simply had to shake the Symphony Society out of its complacence, its assumption that things could be done just as they had always been done, its comfortable conviction that the musicians had no choice but to continue accepting half-time work and poor pay.

We had several orchestra meetings to work out our demands in late 1964 and early 1965. There were always some who were ready to push for what we really wanted and knew we deserved, others who were reluctant to "demand" at all, preferring to ask only for what looked easily possible of attainment.

We had to bring people together on a program the whole orchestra would be willing to fight for—even strike for, if necessary—and there had never been a strike in the history of the St. Louis Symphony. When we had achieved such unity, the Orchestra Committee transmitted our contract proposals to the Union, which passed them on to the Symphony Society.

We demanded a 52-week season at a minimum salary of $200 a week. Some smaller but still important changes were proposed, such as one full day off without travel or service in every tour week, an increase in the per diem on tour, and an increase in the personnel of the orchestra to a minimum of 90.

The Committee worked actively to keep all players informed, to maintain orchestral unity, to work closely with officers of the Local Union, to spread the word in the community. Henry Loew (principal bass) was Committee Chair. The other members were Israel Borouchoff (flute), Mel Jernigan (trombone) and two other members of the bass section, Joe Kleeman and myself.

It might seem strange that three of the five were from the bass section. However, not only in St. Louis, but in other orchestras as well, bass players are often active in the collective work of advancing the interests of the musicians. We are not frustrated soloists and sometimes refer to ourselves as "gang players." This makes for cooperation and a recognition that the welfare of one depends on the welfare of all.

The Local Union Board was in agreement with the Orchestra. President Ken Farmer and the Orchestra Committee were the negotiating team.

The union demands were placed before the Society in February of 1965, early enough to provide time for negotiations and planning before the end of the 1964-65 season. But the Society did not respond until April, when the season was almost over and many of the players would be leaving town in search of summer work.

The Society's counter-proposal did not even come within shouting distance of our demands. We were offered a $5 increase in the minimum and a one-week addition to the season. This represented a step back from the pace of improvement set in the previous contract.

There may have been some members of the orchestra who really thought we could win a 54% increase in pay and a 22-week increase in the season in one contract. We on the Committee knew that eventually we would have to compromise. We wanted a commitment out of the Symphony Society on our goal, however, and a big step toward it immediately. To get that, we had to be prepared to hang tough for all of it as long as we could. At this point, the Society was not even taking us seriously.

When the Union Board rejected the Society's offer, the Society made no effort to negotiate but simply repeated the offer in June in a letter to the Union and to each individual musician, threatening to cancel the season if it were not accepted.

We were prepared for that cancellation threat and were not going to allow the fear of losing the season to be the determining factor this time. We wanted to get down to negotiations, but the summer dragged along with the Society apparently believing that the months with no action on a new contract would wear us down.

Quite the contrary, things were happening that summer in other orchestras that strengthened our resolve. On August 5, the Minneapolis Orchestra signed a five-year contract increasing the season to 45 weeks in the final year, with a minimum of $205 a week.

Chicago was also in negotiations. Early in September they concluded their contract and sent us an editorial from the *Chicago Sun-Times*, headed "Another Chicago First." The editorial hailed "a new era of economic well-being and security for the 105 men and women of the Chicago Orchestra. A five-year contract has been signed guaranteeing a rising scale of income and benefits culminating in a minimum of $245 weekly for 52 weeks."

My old friend Fred Batchelder, Chairman of the Philadelphia Orchestra Committee, wrote to say, "Having been through many grim struggles to raise our salary to a minimum of $12,400 per year, the members of the Philadelphia Orchestra wholeheartedly support our colleagues in the St. Louis Symphony in their difficult task of gaining a decent contract."

We were also encouraged by the fact that the Arts Council, which supplied about half the Symphony's budget, was doing better in its current fund drive than before. When we did sit down to talk, the Society's position was that what we were asking was financially impossible. Stanley Goodman, the department store executive who was the Society president, wanted us to know that he was the musicians' friend. He didn't dispute our contention that we deserved what we were asking. It was just that to his great sorrow, he couldn't meet our demands.

On our side of the table, Henry as Committee Chair was our prime spokesman throughout. In negotiations, he was so convincing in describing the musicians' plight that he could almost make our opponents cry. Borouchoff was good with figures, quick to grasp everything thrown at us and catch each flaw in it. When they handed us columns of figures to show what a difficult financial situation the Symphony faced, Izzy ran his finger down the first column and immediately pointed out an error. Joe Kleeman spoke little, but very much to the point when he did speak. Union president Farmer also made our case well, both in negotiations and in speaking to the press.

So the management team did not overpower us, though it did represent St. Louis money. In addition to Goodman, there were investment banker Orrin Wightman, Al Fleischman, head of a big advertising agency, other members of the Symphony Board; and, of course, Manager William Zalken.

When we refused to accept their contention that the Society could do no better than their "last word" in the spring, Fleischman lost his temper and cursed us out. Apparently his colleagues realized that this was unacceptable behavior, as he was seemingly dropped from their team.

Finally, they came up with what they called their "final offer," saying "acceptance or rejection will determine whether we can go ahead with next season." This time they proposed a three-year contract increasing the season two weeks each of the first two years and one the third year and raising the minimum $10 each of the first two years and $5 the third.

This was a considerable improvement over the previous offer and showed up the bogus finality of the earlier one. However, it was not good enough and addressed none of the other issues. Orchestra members refused to regard the offer as an ultimatum. When the Society insisted on a ratification vote, several players put together a "vote no" letter to their colleagues that concluded:

> The Symphony Society's job is to run an orchestra. Their stated goal is to make St. Louis one of the "top five" orchestras in the country. They can't just talk about these things. We have an opportunity to encourage them to do their job. There are many things we can do. The first is, of course, to unanimously reject their preliminary proposal.

The Union mailed the management offer to all orchestra members. It was defeated by a vote of 46 to 16. We recognized the risk of losing weeks of work and pay if it came to a strike, but the loss would be temporary, the gains would be permanent.

By September 9, with the season opening less than a month away, we decided it was time to compromise. This is always a difficult decision. When can you get more by hanging tough? When have you pushed management as far as they will go? We had gained a little, and sixteen orchestra members had been willing to settle. On the other hand, a faction was adamantly opposed to any compromise.

We held an orchestra meeting to discuss it and agreed to lower our demands to $188 a week for a 50-week season. The Society responded by offering one more week for a total of 33— a week that would be paid for by the new State Arts Council. They announced that unless this offer was accepted within a few days, the entire season would be cancelled.

Another orchestra meeting was called. The membership rejected this third "final offer." The union refused to submit it to the membership in another mailed ballot, since a majority had already expressed opposition.

Although the season was not scheduled to begin for almost a month and therefore we were not officially on strike, we had not had contracts since the close of the previous season in May. The threat of a season cancellation had been present since June. There were no further negotiations. We felt we were already on strike.

Tension increased throughout September. The Society cancelled the kick-off for the season ticket campaign and thereafter cried the blues because ticket sales were not going well.

An unnamed "Symphony spokesman" was quoted in the press downplaying our need for a substantial raise by stating that "some players make up to $300 a week." (Small comfort to the majority of the orchestra on the minimum.) He also claimed that "supplementary work was available to those who seek it." He "doubted that funds could be raised to finance the summer season that would be necessary" to meet our demand for a 50-week season.

But the Symphony, which had seemed to belong to a small group of business and society people, had become the property of the entire community in the course of the summer and early fall. More and more people were agreeing with the musicians' contention that allowing the Symphony to collapse would seriously erode the cultural life of the city. One disgruntled concert-goer said it would turn St. Louis into a "mud hole on the banks of the Mississippi."

Kay Drey, music lover and friend of musicians, had put together a four-page "Facts of the Symphony Crisis" during the summer, which indicated support for the musicians' demands for year-round work and higher pay. She pointed out the following ways to raise the larger budget required: Full-time management, a revitalized endowment fund, increased efforts to complete or surpass the current Arts Council fund drive, additional ticket revenue through more summer concerts and other musical events, and possible subsidies by city, county, state, and federal governments.

Mrs. Drey set out to raise $1,000 each from 100 people, convinced that support for the Symphony was much broader than had ever been tapped.

Wives of symphony musicians and close friends began to reach out into the community. The result was the formation of a Committee to Save Our Symphony (S.O.S.). It made itself known with a paid advertisement in the *St. Louis Post-Dispatch* on Monday, September 20. Beside a line drawing of half a violin was the heading:

> YOU CAN'T MAKE VIOLIN MUSIC ON HALF AN INSTRUMENT. YOU CAN'T MAKE SYMPHONY MUSIC ON HALF A PROFESSIONAL SALARY.
>
> We can't allow our Symphony to die. Not only our concert pleasure is at stake, but the musical education of our children, the reputation of our city, the future of our cultural life . . . We urge the Symphony Society to reconsider its refusal to compromise, and both sides to negotiate until an agreement is reached.

S.O.S. held a public meeting at Fontbonne College and voted to raise $20,000, including the more than $7,000 already raised by Mrs. Drey. A weekend phone campaign was set up to obtain pledges. One couple with a home fronting Delmar Boulevard, a main city-county street, put a large "Save Our Symphony" sign in their yard. A TV station filmed people going up the walk to make their contributions.

Kay Drey and Alberta Slavin (an S.O.S. leader who later became a well-known consumer advocate) were welcomed into the Union office for joint efforts.

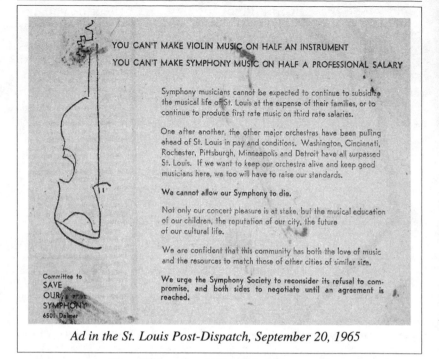

YOU CAN'T MAKE VIOLIN MUSIC ON HALF AN INSTRUMENT

YOU CAN'T MAKE SYMPHONY MUSIC ON HALF A PROFESSIONAL SALARY

Symphony musicians cannot be expected to continue to subsidize the musical life of St. Louis at the expense of their families, or to continue to produce first rate music on third rate salaries.

One after another, the other major orchestras have been pulling ahead of St. Louis in pay and conditions. Washington, Cincinnati, Rochester, Pittsburgh, Minneapolis and Detroit have all surpassed St. Louis. If we want to keep our orchestra alive and keep good musicians here, we too will have to raise our standards.

We cannot allow our Symphony to die.

Not only our concert pleasure is at stake, but the musical education of our children, the reputation of our city, the future of our cultural life.

We are confident that this community has both the love of music and the resources to match those of other cities of similar size.

Committee to
SAVE
OUR
SYMPHONY
6501 Delmar

We urge the Symphony Society to reconsider its refusal to compromise, and both sides to negotiate until an agreement is reached.

Ad in the St. Louis Post-Dispatch, September 20, 1965

An anonymous financier called the Union with an offer to raise the money that separated the two sides. A telegram was sent to the Society by the *Cardinals*, the professional football club, offering to play pre-season games for the benefit of the Symphony in 1966 and 1967. Film-maker Charles Guggenheim offered to put on a benefit premier showing of his film, "The Fisherman and His Soul."

Another element in the situation was that the Symphony crisis had become front-page news day after day. The public agitation and support had made the news and had generated quite a number of letters to the editor. Almost all expressed dismay at the thought of losing the orchestra and many were in support of the musicians. In one case, a man who wrote in defense of the Society was answered by his brother who supported the musicians.

Various proposals were offered by the letter-writers, ranging from the ridiculous to the practical. One suggested that "Since the musicians are asking a full year's pay, possibly the symphony could give it to them and place them on full-time employment. Any income from teaching or outside engagements would go directly to the Society rather than to the musicians." Another suggested a small tax in city and county, while a third pointed out that "there are many wealthy and prosperous business and civic-minded leaders who can well afford to guarantee the necessary funds." He was ready to single out "one of our larger corporations whose primary source of business is derived from federal contracts . . . from which tremendous profits are being realized."

The Eastern Missouri Psychiatric Society urged increased community support for the Symphony endowment fund, saying the cancellation of the season would have a severe "emotional and psychological impact on the community."

The president of the St. Louis County Art Association proposed that each leading St. Louis area suburban community support one summer concert each week for ten weeks.

Of the two St. Louis daily papers, the *Globe-Democrat* continued throughout to take the Society position. *The Post-Dispatch*, although always acknowledging that the musicians deserved better, concluded on September 9 that "we do not see how the Symphony Society is in a financial position to make much more of an offer." We therefore started the September negotiating sessions with both papers against us.

However, the public outcry, the quiet reasonableness of Kay Drey, who talked with one of the editorial writers, and the influence of music critic Thomas Sherman, wrought a change in the *Post-Dispatch* editorial policy.

After reprinting a piece from the *New York Times* reporting that "the trend of major orchestras is to provide musicians with year-round work," the paper expressed continued doubt about the city's ability to meet the musicians' demands but noted that "eventually St. Louis will have to conform to the national trend."

Mayor Cervantes said it is "unthinkable that the city should lose this cultural asset," and County Supervisor Lawrence Roos said the loss of the symphony would be "a serious blow to the entire metropolitan area." Roos urged both sides to continue seeking "common ground."

Louis Nauman, Union secretary, wrote a long letter to the press correcting misinformation in a *Globe-Democrat* piece and saying that the musicians, "by working for low wages, have subsidized the Symphony long enough."

In an effort to get negotiations going again, Farmer asked the Arts Council to mediate the dispute. Goodman agreed—

how could he not?—and negotiations resumed on September 23 with W. MacLean Johnson, Arts Council president, Merrimon Cuninggim, executive director of the Danforth Foundation, and Homer E. Sayad, president of the Opera Theater, sitting in.

The Committee to Save Our Symphony adopted a resolution that was sent to the Society, the Union, and the press expressing "hope that the present negotiations will be fruitful" and pledging "to do our utmost to meet the challenge" of Symphony support "with new ideas, greater efforts and additional financial support."

On September 26 Sherman had a long piece pointing out the "obvious remedy" which "lies with the people of St. Louis and more particularly with the leading citizens of the community who regard a symphony orchestra as an essential part of the city's cultural apparatus."

Two days later, a *Post-Dispatch* editorial suggested that "Surely there is a reasonable basis for compromise."

When it became obvious that the Society would not budge, we on the Union side of the table made a major effort to bridge the gap. We would agree to much less than we had been asking, if the Symphony would agree to a one-year contract. We proposed $156 a week for a 35-week season. This was approximately what the Society had proposed to achieve in three years.

The Symphony refused to consider a one-year contract. The only concession they offered

THE LOST CHORD

St. Louis Post-Dispatch
cartoon, September 20, 1965

was upping the salary in the first year another five dollars, and agreeing to one more week in the first season.

A full-time manager would be hired as the union had been urging, and a "growth clause" would be added to the contract, which would express their determination to move forward, and, in case of success in raising additional funds, to share these with the musicians. Hiring a full-time manager was definitely a good sign, but the growth clause was too vague to mean much.

After three days of negotiations, including a 12-hour session on Saturday, September 25, the mediators gave up, offering to try again if either party felt they might be helpful. W. MacLean Johnson said the irony of the situation was that the season was being threatened at a high point in the orchestra's history.

Goodman, interviewed by the *Post-Dispatch*, spoke about increased ticket sales the previous season, greater support for the Arts Council, and other hopeful signs. Yet he claimed none of this was enough to meet the orchestra's demands.

On Saturday, October 2, the Symphony Society cancelled the season. We on the Committee worked out a statement on our position. It was published in full in the *Post-Dispatch* on October 3.

"We are now in an unfortunate state of crisis. We are about to bury the second oldest orchestra in the country. The Symphony Society had two alternatives; one was to start the concert season on Tuesday on a one-year basis with full awareness of the tremendous interest and money pouring in from the community . . . The other . . . to cancel the season."

We pointed out that "With the symphony no longer a reality, public support can hardly be expected to show confidence in the long-term future. A dead issue cannot cry for help. It is the society's civic responsibility to bring about a revival of the issue, while there is still time."

We called the Society's bluff on their claim that the five-week spring tour had to be canceled the previous Friday. We had checked with Columbia Artists Management and learned there was still considerable time. We also sent telegrams appealing to the Mayor and the County Supervisor to bring the two sides together.

One day before the scheduled date of the first rehearsal the Mayor called Society president Goodman and Union president Farmer to his office. Henry accompanied Farmer. The Mayor was not depending on sweet reason to bridge the gap between Society and Union. He had something else in mind. This requires a word or two of background.

Mayor Alfonso J. Cervantes was looked on as an outsider by the people who had been accustomed to run the city and the county and especially by the society people who had always considered the Symphony both their burden and their private preserve.

Cervantes had become convinced of the necessity and the popularity of saving the symphony. He also had ideas of his own about promoting the city. One of them was an organization called the St. Louis Ambassadors, business people concerned with attracting industry and tourism to St. Louis. Like the Mayor himself, they were outside the inner circle, which included the Symphony Society. Perhaps he rather liked the idea of bringing his Ambassadors to the rescue of the upper crust. When Cervantes had both sides in his office, he said he was authorized by the Ambassadors to offer $100,000 over three years to bridge the gap between the two sides.

The Union agreed to a three-year contract and to one less week in the first year than we had been asking, and to no greater increase in the season in successive years than the Symphony had already conceded—two the second year, one the third year. The Symphony agreed to one week more the first year. Ambassador money was to bring salaries up to $156 the first year—our last offer—to $171 the second year, and to $181 the third year.

Goodman accepted the plan with understandable reluctance. Not only was he uncomfortable with being forced into a corner where he had to agree, but he could probably see ahead to the end of the three-year contract when the musicians would begin bargaining for more on the basis of a $181 minimum already achieved. The orchestra met the next day and voted to accept the deal. The season seemed to be saved; the strike was off the very day it was to start!

However, with salary and length of season agreed, we were now ready to bargain on the other issues: a full day off during each tour week, an increase in the per diem on tour, an increase in the personnel from 87 to 90, and other minor matters.

Goodman's response was that the musicians had voted on a contract that they were to "accept or reject as offered with no further negotiation."

The next day, Goodman backed out of the agreement reached in the Mayor's office, and we were on strike after all, or rather were locked out.

There appeared little hope of saving the season. The Arts Council had tried to bring the two sides together and failed. Now it felt that its own existence was in jeopardy, the Symphony being the largest of the nine cultural institutions included in it. The Mayor was reported to be blaming the musicians for destroying the settlement he had worked out.

Unity had been strong throughout the summer and well into the tense days of September. Now it was eroding. The weapon of fear was affecting some performers who

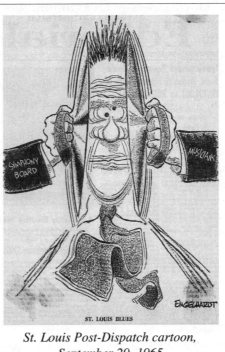

St. Louis Post-Dispatch cartoon, September 29, 1965

saw their jobs disappearing. They felt that all was now lost and that once having succeeded in getting substantial concessions from the Society on pay and length of season, the other issues should not have been allowed to stand in the way.

On the other hand, there were orchestra members who felt that the Union and the Committee should not have agreed to such a major reduction of the original demands and should not have presented an agreement to the orchestra with so much unsettled.

This made it particularly difficult for those of us on the Committee. It is one thing to lead a united effort by a hopeful orchestra even when negotiations are difficult and contentious. It is another to continue to lead when you are getting criticism from all sides and it begins to look like a failed effort.

The settlement in the Mayor's office had been hailed by the *Post-Dispatch* with some criticism of the Union for its previous "obstinacy." When the Society backed out, however, the paper called its position "incomprehensible" and the Union's position "eminently fair."

Our success in breaking through the media barrier was crucial to our ultimate success, but it was one of our community contacts that proved to be the key to breaking the impasse. An aide to the Mayor had ties to some of the professional people in S.O.S., Professor Barry Commoner of Washington University, the well-known environmental scientist, in particular. A little backstage maneuvering took place.

The Mayor was persuaded to make another effort. The Society backed up and agreed to most of the conditions they had been claiming they would no longer accept. We in the Union agreed to a contract with all of our minor issues untouched. We also agreed to a season that would not begin until early November in order to give the Society the time they claimed to need to gear up. It would therefore not include the full 34 weeks we had on paper.

The orchestra voted to accept. The contract was signed. The fight was over. The lockout had lasted only one week, although it seemed that we had been on strike for months.

What had we gained? Even with the season shortened at the front end, minimum players would make more this season than in the previous one, while the succeeding years would bring us to a 37-week season and an annual salary of $6,697.

What was perhaps even more important, we had made the Society and the whole community aware that we were determined to get professional pay for professional performances.

The first concert of the 1965-66 season was a humdinger!

OUR FAMILY/OUR CITY

We had not been living in St. Louis long before we became concerned that our children were growing up in an environment of bricks and cement. Picnics in Forest Park were all very well but no substitute for roaming freely through woods and hills as both Virginia and I had done as children.

We spent most of our free time one summer in the mid-fifties looking for a place in the country, not to replace but to supplement our city home. We drew a circle with our home at the center and a radius of sixty miles. We wanted to be close enough to the city so that even a one-day trip would be practical.

It soon became obvious that the piece of our circle on the east side of the Mississippi in Illinois was mostly flat and covered with small towns and farms. Missouri southwest of St. Louis looked most promising.

We expected that an acre or two would be the most we could afford but found that any piece of land that small was either farm land or a piece of a recreational development and in either case was out of our range. However, there were some large tracts of woodland where the price per acre was low. We drove up and down many country roads and finally found what we wanted.

It was a 240-acre tract, forty acres wide, with a creek running down the middle. The 40 acres at the end gave it an L shape. Too rocky and hilly to be good farmland, most of it had been logged off about twenty years previously. It was now covered with predominantly oak second-growth forest. The most remote forty acres had not even been logged.

The idea that we could be owners of that much land was mind-boggling, but it was only nineteen dollars an acre. We scraped up the last penny of our small savings and managed to make the down payment. We needed a new car but couldn't have both that and a country place. The old wreck we were driving broke down on the way to sign the papers but we managed to revive it and keep it going a few more years.

Rocky Branch in summer . . .

. . . and in winter

"Rocky Branch," as we called our place from the name of the little creek, contributed immensely to the health and pleasure of our whole family. Many of our friends enjoyed it as well.

Marc pushing Russell in the hammock

By 1960, we were feeling constricted in our small apartment in town. Marc was outgrowing the built-in youth bed in his room, and the room was too small for a larger bed. I had no adequate workshop for my instrument repair work. At times one of the children would complain at bedtime, "Daddy, I can't go to bed. There's a bass fiddle on my bed, *again.*"

Walter and Essie agreed to a new house hunt. We found what we wanted at 4393 Westminster Place, which had once

Enjoying Rocky Branch food

been the fashionable west end of St. Louis. The estates of Ladue and other suburbs had long since upstaged it. It was now another "changing neighborhood." Few African-American home buyers were able to afford these big mansions, while most white homebuyers stupidly shunned changing neighborhoods, so there were some real bargains to be had.

We bought a three-story brick house with five baths and eight fireplaces for $15,500—half of what our friends were paying for "little boxes on the hillside" in the suburbs. Walter and Essie had the first floor and we had the two upper floors, splitting the cost one-third for them and two-thirds for us, instead of half-and-half as at Labadie.

4393 Westminster Place, with Cynthia's tower room on the upper-right

Cynthia laid claim to a third floor room with a corner tower, while Marc, after exploring the entire house in the hope of finding some secret hiding places, was satisfied with a room about three times the size of his Labadie quarters.

On Labadie we had shared one entrance. Now each family had a private entrance. The Johnsons used the front door and we a side door that opened onto a hall and a staircase leading to our floors.

Another staircase went up from the front hall. We removed it, giving the Johnsons more room. We covered over the stairwell with a raised platform that gave us a stage for chamber music. Several times musicians who were preparing to give recitals or solo with the Little Symphony played a rehearsal there. We and our friends were the preview audience.

Especially memorable was the concert we put on after the strike as a "thank you" to some of the people outside the orchestra who had been so helpful. We did the *Trout* (of course), and three harpists played a number together, a most unusual and beautiful performance.

I now had ample space for my workshop on the third floor in what had previously been a storeroom. The original owners of the house had been the Maestre family. Although it had passed through other hands before reaching us, the large drawers in this storeroom were still labeled "Mr. Maestre's summer straw hats," "Mr. Maestre's hunting togs," etc.

Showing friends through the house one day, we discovered that the kids had changed one label to read simply "Mr. Maestre."

The so-called ballroom, also on the third floor, was big enough for a ping-pong table. Marc became such an addict that he met friends at the door as soon as they rang the bell, with the greeting, "Want to play ping-pong?"

Cynthia and Marc were growing up to be wonderful kids, so our family life was a happy one. With a good marriage, two such children, socially useful jobs we enjoyed doing, a fine house in town and a place in the country, how could we want anything more?

We did want more. We wanted peace in the world, and it didn't look like we were going to get it any time soon. The shadow of nuclear war hung over the world. We had campaigned against the H-bomb, circulated the Stockholm Peace Appeal, expressed our opposition to the Korean War, but there was more to do. The movement for peace and disarmament remained small, and the war danger continued to grow.

Barry Commoner alerted us to the fact that not only war itself, but preparations for war were a serious danger. Nuclear tests, exploded in the atmosphere, were spreading radioactive fallout far beyond the Pacific and Nevada test sites.

Together with his colleagues, physicist John Fowler, pathologist Walter Bauer and others, Barry was trying to educate citizens about the fallout danger. We joined with them and other concerned people in 1958 to found a scientist-citizen organization called the St. Louis Citizens Committee for Nuclear Information (CNI). Gloria Commoner became its first executive secretary.

It was a difficult organization for the un-Americans to target since it was not the usual activist organization and took no political positions. Its purpose was to provide citizens with the scientific information they needed on the political issues of the nuclear age. Nevertheless, there are times when nothing is more subversive of establishment positions than the truth.

Virginia was on the CNI Board, serving as its secretary for several years. CNI was a coalition of scientists, writers, environmentalists and aware citizens. Virginia had come to believe that a grave danger to humanity was the degradation of the environment. At a meeting of people with similar concerns, she gave forth on her views, which were well received. Barry Commoner said to Virginia, "Go home and write it up—and don't joggle your head on the way."

As the organization grew and its mimeographed newsletter, *Nuclear Information*, attracted subscribers far beyond St. Louis, CNI got some grant support. This made it possible to enlarge the newsletter into a magazine and hire a fulltime editor. Virginia left the ILGWU early in 1962 to take on that job, which she held until mid-1969. She saw the publication through several changes, from *Nuclear Information* to *Scientist and Citizen* and then to *Environment* as its scope widened to include other environmental problems.

In 1963, the Civil Rights Movement had its first major impact on St. Louis in the case of the St. Louis Committee for Racial Equality (CORE) vs. the Jefferson Bank. This bank was located in the African-American community but had an almost entirely white work force.

We were not among those who picketed the bank and went to jail in this effort to get black workers hired, or who went to jail simply because they were officers of CORE, but we supported the cause. We put up our house, with Walter and Essie's agreement, to guarantee bail. Virginia and I attended the ensuing court hearings. The proceedings were rather dull and seemed to drag on endlessly. A lunch break never seemed to arrive. One of the lawyers finally interrupted and informed the judge that the clock was quite slow and that in actuality the lunch break was overdue. His honor pointed to the clock and said, "The clocks in this building are all on one circuit. The *whole system* is out of whack." A voice piped up from the back of the room: "Right on, your honor!" Laughter and applause erupted.

Virginia wrote an article for *Focus*, a local magazine about the Jefferson Bank case, which made an important contribution to clarifying the issues. They had been considerably muddied in the press.

The intransigence of the bank, the unfair handling of the case (Millsap, the bank's attorney, was appointed by the court as special prosecutor) and the harsh sentences meted out by Judge Scott rocked the city. Efforts were made to divide African-American leaders into "responsible" and "irresponsible" according to whether or not they approved of challenging a court restraining order.

Such efforts failed. As one such leader remarked wryly, "Millsap and Judge Scott have made the greatest contribution to Negro unity in St. Louis in twenty years."

One of those who went to jail was Alderman William Clay. Not long after, he was elected to his first term in Congress where he eventually became one of the senior members of the House.

Thirty African-American leaders signed a "Declaration of Civic Concern and Unity to the City of St. Louis." It said in part, "The Jefferson Bank controversy serves to highlight the great need for immediate steps to insure democratic hiring practices in the metropolitan St. Louis area." The Declaration pointed out "that the average income ($3,700) of a Negro family is only half that of the average white family; that the unemployment of Negroes is three times that of whites, and that housing available to Negroes is generally substandard, congested, and restricted." [22]

The Conference on Religion and Race, in which Protestant, Catholic and Jewish faiths were linked, called for a procession for interracial justice.

Held on November 24, the procession became a memorial for President Kennedy, who had been assassinated two days before, as well as an affirmation of belief in interracial justice and equal opportunity. It drew 35,000 people, and was by far the most racially integrated demonstration the city had ever seen.

Neither the intensity of those weeks, nor the unity then developed could be maintained at the same level. Nevertheless, St. Louis was never quite the same again.

Changes were taking place throughout the country. The Civil Rights upsurge was the most striking but not the only example of greater political activism and less fear than in the dreadful 1950s. It was no accident that the musicians were more militant than they had been for years. With the discrediting of McCarthy, the collapse of the Smith Act prosecutions, and the Partial Test Ban Treaty, it became possible to act more effectively in unions, peace and civil rights organizations.

The Vietnam War at first seemed to many people a minor affair in a faraway country of which they had never heard. As it began to draw more and more young men into the draft and more of them came home in body bags, it elicited more and more opposition throughout the country. The war escalated in intensity; every weapon short of nuclear bombs was thrown at Vietnam, and some hawks even called for the use of the nuclear "option."

We participated in petitions and demonstrations against the war. Marc was old enough to join us, and Cynthia, away at Reed College, participated in student actions on her campus. The longer the war went on, the broader and more vocal the

opposition became. In the spring of 1972, I drew up a letter opposing the war to be sent to the two Missouri senators, Eagleton and Symington, and circulated it through the orchestra. A majority signed, including the entire bass section and some others who would never previously sign anything political.

Cynthia graduated from Reed in 1965 and went to work with Virginia for a year as a secretary but with the purpose of learning editorial work. All through the next months we planned a trip to Europe for the summer of 1966. We pinned a map of Europe up on the dining room wall and put a can with a slot in the top underneath it for spare nickels.

Cynthia at Reed College, Portland, Oregon

*Cynthia and the Land
Rover in Europe*

If someone wanted so much as a package of chewing gum, I would say, "O.K., buy your gum. We won't go to Europe, but at least you'll have your chewing gum."

Marc chose Mont Ste Michel as the thing he most wanted to see, and Cynthia chose the Winged Victory at the Louvre in Paris.

I didn't sign up for the Little Symphony so we could spend the whole summer on the trip. Virginia arranged to have two months off without pay in addition to her regular month's vacation. We ordered a Land Rover, which we picked up when we got to England.

After crossing the channel, we had a delightful time in Paris, the Loire Valley, and—of course—Mont Ste Michel. Then to Switzerland where we picked up the son of friends who had been in school there. Adventures in Italy, Yugoslavia, and Austria followed. We had brought tents, sleeping bags, and a camp stove, and we camped most of the time, alternating with hotel living in some of the cities.

Essie Johnson flew over to Prague to join us for the last month in Czechoslovakia and back across Europe to England, where we boarded the ship for home. It was a memorable experience for all of us. We returned with only five dollars left in our pockets. CNI had obligingly paid Virginia ahead for September-December, and of course that money was gone, too, so we were on short rations. It was well worth it, and the trip was perfectly timed. In earlier years, Marc would not have been ready to enjoy it fully; later, Cynthia would not have been with us. Shortly after we returned, she left home to work for Margaret Mead in New York.

The Communist Party in St. Louis, which had been decimated in the Fifties, began to revive. This was happening all over the country. The government's response, in late 1970 was to frame Angela Davis, a Communist, for murder. Rather than beat the Party back, this had the opposite effect. A defense of

Virginia and Russell at Rocky Branch (early 70s)

Angela Davis built throughout the country and the world in the months that followed. That struggle and her exoneration in June 1972 helped to lift the fog of misrepresentation that had obscured the reality of our program and gave new heart to Communists and non-Communists alike to speak out publicly for their political beliefs.

One event in St. Louis was typical of the change in the atmosphere around the country. As part of Angela's defense, we and several other couples, Party and non-Party, sent out invitations to a dinner to raise money for her legal expenses. We obtained the use of a lovely home in University City. Haywood Burns, one of her lawyers, came to speak. Charlene Clark and Joe Striplin agreed to play some violin duets for the program.

We had such a positive response to

In front of one of many rock walls

Finishing the chimney

the invitation that we had an overflow afternoon tea at our home for those who could not be accommodated at the dinner. A substantial sum was raised for Angela's defense.

STRIKE TWO

When the 1965 strike was over, my feeling was that we had scored an important victory. This assessment was not shared by the entire orchestra. Some considered it a defeat and even accused the Committee of selling out.

In a strike situation, it is important for union negotiators to be backed up by a militant rank and file so that management perceives both the strength this gives the union and the limitations it imposes on compromises. But a refusal to compromise at all or to fail to see real limits on what could be achieved could have driven us into a disastrous situation. We could have lost our community support, and in the end, our season. None of us could possibly know if we could have squeezed out one more concession.

The charge of "sellout" was too much for Henry, who had done a superb job of handling the difficult negotiations while trying to keep the orchestra unified. He stated unequivocally that he was withdrawing from Committee activity.

When the time came to elect the Committee for the 1965-66 season, a letter was circulated through the orchestra urging both Henry and me to run, but he refused.

I did run and received the highest vote among those elected. According to our established procedure, this made me chairman. Some of the others elected were from the dissatisfied faction, so I took the chair over some objections.

I tried to push ahead on some of the unresolved problems, such as the unduly heavy scheduling, especially on tours, and most important, the revision of our inadequate pension plan.

Henry was made Personnel Manager in 1967 in addition to his position as principal bass. This was probably in part a recognition of his intelligence, responsibility, and talent for working with people and in part a move to ensure that he would not return to his previous role as a leader of the musicians. Henry never sacrificed his integrity or his concern for the orchestra as a whole, but his leadership in struggle was missed.

In the season following the strike, it was difficult to accomplish anything with a divided orchestra and a divided Committee. Those who were still smarting from what they considered the defeat of the strike considered themselves the "militants" and were scornful of those they felt were unworthy of that name.

All during my early years in the orchestra, I strove to encourage more militancy in order to give the orchestra a voice, a good loud voice, for our common interests. Militancy, however, is not important for its own sake. The more timid and less vocal have to be encouraged to move forward, and sometimes the more militant have to hold back for the sake of speaking to management with one voice.

I did not run for the Committee the following year but of course remained active in orchestra affairs and a few years later served as chair of the Dismissal Committee.

The following season, negotiations on an improved pension plan continued. The orchestra accepted a new plan in the summer of 1967.

Meanwhile, the Symphony Society took some important steps forward. They hired a full-time manager, later making him executive director and giving him a staff better able to handle publicity and fund raising. Work began toward the development of a substantial endowment fund, something that all major symphonies rely upon and that had been neglected. In the course of the three years, the orchestra had also been increased to 93 members.

Some major bequests and help from the Ford Foundation made it possible for the Society to buy an old movie theater and convert it to a concert hall. Powell Hall gave the Symphony an attractive, permanent home with greatly improved acoustics. It had the advantage for me of being within walking distance of our home on Westminster Place.

The result, according to the Society's figures, was that in the 1967-68 season, a record audience of more than 300,000 heard the concerts. The larger audience and an increase in ticket prices brought a 34% increase in income from ticket sales. The Symphony also enjoyed a 41% increase in income from the Arts and Education Fund.

We in the orchestra felt that this was a good basis for another major step forward in pay and length of season. As the three-year contract that concluded the 1965 strike approached its end in the spring of 1968, dissatisfaction with our unfinished business grew. The orchestra came together around our determination to take another substantial step toward the goal of year-round work and a living wage. Whether it was seen as building on our 1965 accomplishments or as achieving what should have been accomplished then was less important than unity around our new demands. Better music would be one of the results.

Negotiations, which should have begun in the spring of 1968, were held up by a protracted disagreement between the Symphony Society and the local union over the question of hiring local musicians. This was still not settled when the 1968-69 season started in the fall. We opened the season without a contract, with the understanding that when agreement was reached, it would be effective as of the season's opening.

On September 9, when the hiring problem was finally settled and negotiations on the new contract began, the Orchestra asked for a one-year contract with a 45-week season and a $250 per week minimum.

We wanted to start where we left off at the end of the 1967-68 season, but management had always considered the additional weeks that had been paid for by the St. Louis Ambassadors and the "take" at special football games by the *Cardinals* as extras. So their basis for negotiating improvements started with what they called the "guaranteed minimum."

The Society's response to us was an offer of 38 weeks, with the minimum to rise to $188.50 the first season (an annual salary of $7,163) with small additional raises in two successive seasons, bringing the annual salary to $7,547.

There were two bass players on the Committee: Bob Maisel, Chairman, and Terry Kippenberger; two trombone players, Bernard Schneider and Melvyn Jernigan; and Bobby Swain, violinist. In the negotiations, they agreed to a three-year contract and offered other concessions, while management improved its offer to an annual salary of $8,022.

The Committee and the Union found it impossible to move management significantly on the main issues. After playing four weeks without a contract, we voted to strike.

"Musicians applaud you and thank you for the support that has rebuilt this hall and filled it with enthusiastic audiences," said a letter from the orchestra written with Virginia's help and handed out to concert-goers by musicians' wives as people gathered for the October 13 subscription concert.

"We don't want to stop making music. It's our profession. It's our life. We have played for four weeks under our old contract in the hope that neither you nor we would have to miss a note." The letter went on to say the audience deserved an explanation of why "we are forced to lay down our instruments tomorrow." The reason given was that management's last offer was for an annual salary "$3,600 less than the average of the top ten American orchestras."

Once on strike, we picketed the hall in our concert clothes, which attracted some national media attention. Fortunately for us, the *Post-Dispatch* was rather friendly throughout the strike, although we had lost music critic Thomas Sherman, who died that year.

St. Louis Symphony Orchestra strike, 1968

The Save Our Symphony organization supported us, coming up with a suggestion for selling "shares" in a summer season to business leaders, labor unions and others to finance a free six-week summer season in the park. This was dismissed out of hand by the Society as contrary to the Symphony's agreement with the Arts Fund not to conduct separate fund raising endeavors.

In general, however, the Society conducted itself much differently from 1965, when it had antagonized the community. There were no threats to cancel the season. They did negotiate on some things such as scheduling and per diem on tour instead of stonewalling on all the minor issues.

The Committee issued a publicity statement indicating that what separated the two sides was the $200,000 it would take to bring the pay up and lengthen the season, saying, "We are confident that the necessary $200,000 difference will be found and that one of the nation's oldest cultural and educational organizations will continue to be of service to the community."

A few days later, there was a free chamber concert on the steps of the Old Post Office, with brass and wind players from the Symphony performing. Later in the strike, we put on a full symphony concert, with the audience contributing to benefit the musicians in greatest need. These events helped to keep the strike and its issues before the public.

Perhaps more of a community response was expected by the Committee, similar to what had happened in 1965. That was unrealistic. Community support is important in any strike and particularly so in one which directly involves the public, like a symphony, a retail store or chain, or a hospital. However, it takes time and a lot of work to build that support. In most cases, what is sought is moral support and perhaps contributions to a strike fund but not the kind of money that was separating the Orchestra and the Society.

There were important differences between 1965 and 1968. Although the actual weeks on strike were less in 1965, we were in a pre-strike situation throughout the spring and summer, which gave us more time to build community support. The abysmal salaries of that time came as something of a shock, not only to concert goers but also to others in the community. This brought us sympathy while the Society's cancellation of the season made the situation urgent.

When it came to the big money, the mayor had been the key, but it was the vocal support of the community and the threat of losing the orchestra that gave him a basis for intervening.

When we had been on strike a week in 1968, the Society made a new offer. Southern Illinois University had proposed a six-week outdoor season on their Edwardsville campus. The Society offered to increase the season to 42 weeks, but that was only four weeks more than their original offer, not the six the summer season would add. The orchestra rejected it. The Society broke off negotiations.

There was no movement for almost two weeks. It became exceedingly difficult to maintain unity and keep morale high. Since I was not on the Committee, I did not have the same responsibility as in the previous strike, but of course I did everything I could. We had a social get-together in our home for as many of the musicians and their spouses as wanted to come, as we had done in 1965. We continued to work for community support.

Finally, the Symphony Society let it be known through the press that they were ready to talk, and negotiations were resumed. There was no change from the last offer on the minimum: It was to be $195 the first year, $200 the second year, and $205 the third year. However, the Society agreed to increase the length of season to 44, 47, and 49 weeks.

This was presented to the Orchestra and accepted by a vote of 57 to 19.

A major second step toward year-round work and a livable salary had been won. The Society had also agreed to confer with the orchestra on health insurance to go into effect not later than January 1, 1969, although they would not commit to more than $5,000 a year for this purpose. We musicians had to contribute to our health insurance for the first few years.

There was another first in the new contract: a week's vacation. It was a mere token, as it was to include either Christmas or New Year's Day.

Beginning in 1971, with the next contract, St. Louis musicians as well as those in other orchestras received legal assistance in negotiations through ICSOM. By this time the struggles that had been carried on in other orchestras as well as ours and the growing strength of ICSOM were changing the nature of symphonic work throughout the country.

The 1971 two-year contract made the Society responsible for the full cost of both health insurance and pensions. It lengthened the season in the second year to 51 weeks and provided four weeks of paid vacation in 1971-72 and six weeks the following year.

The Committee that negotiated it was competently chaired by Larry Strieby, a horn player who joined the orchestra in 1967. Also on the Committee was another new addition, Brad

Buckley (contrabassoon). Brad has since played a large part in both St. Louis Symphony and ICSOM affairs.

This concluded what was probably the most significant decade in the symphony's history.

Sometimes I think . . . but often nothing comes of it.

SYMPHONIC SOLIDARITY
Overture, Basses :: Coda, Full Orchestra

In the fall of 1972, as my sixtieth birthday approached, I began my twenty-fourth season with the St. Louis Symphony. I fully expected to stay right there until I reached sixty-five, and then challenge the now-you're-sixty-five-it's-time-to-retire dictum the management was using. It was not that I particularly wanted to play until I was seventy, I just thought it was time to break the automatic retirement at sixty-five tradition. Musicians of that age are often well able to play, sometimes at the peak of their powers.

The Orchestra was now able to attract and keep excellent musicians and was playing concerts of which we could all be proud. A Washington, D.C. concert the previous season had brought a review calling our performance "glorious" and the orchestra "a flexible ensemble, instant in response, and handsome in tone."

Walter Susskind, our conductor since 1968, returned from guest conducting in Philadelphia, where he had spoken to musicians there of his satisfaction with our orchestra, mentioning the bass section in particular.

It was a good section. Henry was a superb principal. He and I had shared the first stand since 1950 and hardly needed words to communicate as we played together. The whole section had been playing together for ten years with only one change, when Warren Claunch left for the service and was replaced by Richard Muehlmann. Claunch was now back in the section, and Muehlmann was still with us, so we had nine basses capable of producing a great sound.

One aspect of that sound was that over the years Henry put considerable emphasis on good instruments. His own was a fine Gabrielli. I have mentioned my Nardelli. Both had come from the famous Wanamaker collection. The rest of the instruments in the section were good to excellent.

The minimum was now up to $215. Although this was a bit beyond the goal we had set back in 1965, inflation was eating up the increases. Nevertheless, we had accomplished a lot. We were finally making a year-round living. Virginia was able to leave her job to devote all her time to writing.

One new contract provision committed the management to notify us by December 1 of an intention not to re-engage for the following season. In effect, it meant that contracts began to be offered about that time.

December 1 came and went and a number of my colleagues had their contracts. Of course, I was not going to be dismissed, but why was I not getting my contract? The answer came on December 12 when I was summoned to a meeting with Conductor Susskind, Executive Director Peter Pastreich and Manager Jim Cain. I found that my battle over ageism had come sooner than I expected.

Pastreich informed me that now that I was gray-haired and approaching retirement age, it was time for me to move back in the section. I would continue to be paid at the same rate ($15 over scale) and could remain until retirement. He went on at some length about other older men who had moved back and how this was common throughout the profession. In his list of musicians who had found it necessary to recognize that age makes a difference, he made the mistake of including our former conductor, Golschmann. Susskind shook his head at this. Conductors were different. He didn't want them brought into the discussion.

Nothing was said to imply that my performance was inadequate or that I was not playing as well as formerly. The only thing even approaching musical criticism was that the conductor "wanted a better sound out of the bass section."

I reminded them of Susskind's previous praise for the section. I discussed my good physical health and high level of energy. They did not disagree, especially as to my energy. Perhaps one of the things they didn't like was the amount of energy I put into struggles for orchestra improvement.

Did they think that if I accepted the demotion and felt the threat of retirement at sixty-five hanging over me, I would be less of a troublemaker? Or that I would so dislike being pushed back in the section that I would leave even before I was 65?

Of course, they didn't say. The whole emphasis was on my age and on their hope and expectation that I would accept the

demotion "gracefully." My response was that I had noticed previously that there was an inordinate pride in the youthfulness
of our orchestra and said I had always been an advocate of a
combination of youth and experience. They were overlooking
the advantage of continuity, I added, questioning whether breaking up the first-stand team would improve the section's sound.
(Maybe it did. My replacement is indeed a superb musician,
Carolyn White.)

"Both Henry and I have exceptionally fine instruments which
is certainly one aspect of the bass sound. We have been playing
together so long that we have developed numerous signals which
make for quick responses and overall good performances," I
said, and added that "It has always surprised me that when a
conductor gets a good section, he wants to dabble in it."

"Mr. Susskind does not dabble," Pastreich replied resent-
fully. Susskind himself said almost nothing except to repeat
several times, "There is nothing more to be said."

I also pointed out truthfully—if not tactfully—that I was the
same age as Susskind, who surely considered himself well able
to continue conducting.

I specifically requested that they rescind the action and give
me my contract as assistant principal for the following season.

The next day, Pastreich wrote to me confirming management's
position and "offering you for 1973-74 a position in the bass
section of the Orchestra, but not a first stand position."

My response was much what it had been in the meeting.

"Throughout my professional career," I said in a letter on
January 1, 1973, "I have felt that arbitrarily pushing a musician back or out after years of service is not only unfair to the
individual musician, but serves neither the cause of good music nor professional stability. It is not surprising, therefore, that
I feel the way I do in my own case. . . I am today a better bass
player than I was either ten or twenty years ago. I continue to
feel that a reshuffling of the basses is not required for the improvement of the section. I remain convinced that as long as
my ability to play is unimpaired, my age, experience and long
record of responsible service to the orchestra rather call for
appreciation and respect from the orchestra management." Again
I proposed that they renew my contract as assistant principal.
Nothing further was said, but I still did not have a contract.

In the spring, there was a concert at Webster College when
Henry was ill and unable to play. I not only played principal but

had the rare experience of a bass solo in one of the numbers. It gave me a renewed feeling of confidence, reinforced by the congratulations of my colleagues.

Then Pastreich posted auditions for the position of assistant principal. He was reckoning without the bass section. There were certainly several members of the section who would have liked to move up, but the section got together (without me) and agreed that no one would audition for what they all regarded as my position. As one of them told me later, they agreed to back me 100%. I also received expressions of concern and support from members of other sections.

Finally, Pastreich let the section know that management was determined to have a new assistant principal. If no one in the section would audition, they would have to look elsewhere. Since they already had nine in the section, while they needed only eight, that would mean some bass players would have to go.

When Bob Maisel pointed out that Pastreich couldn't fire without cause, he said, "Don't worry, I can find a reason."

He then posted the audition announcement a second time. The prospect of advancement had brought no takers; neither did the threat of firing.

At the end of April, Maisel and Jan Roberts, the one woman in the section, received notices of dismissal.

The December deadline being long past, this was a violation of the contract. Whatever "reason" was given, the circumstances made it abundantly clear that it was a trumped-up excuse. Furthermore, singling out Maisel was suspect, since, like me, he had been a frequent and forthright member of the Committee. He had been Chairman during the 1968 strike, and had repeatedly been elected to represent the orchestra in ICSOM. He could be brusque and effective. He was also a well-known jazz bassist.

As we gathered for rehearsal the morning after these dismissal notices were handed out, the musicians reacted with outrage. As soon as the intermission began, there were calls for an emergency orchestra meeting. The Committee called one to begin then and there.

The Committee was instructed to get together with Pastreich immediately and demand the revocation of both dismissals and while they were at it, another one, too. A highly qualified string player had been dismissed but had not contested it. We all felt he was being dismissed because of age, so we wanted him to get his contract as well. He continued to provide valuable service for several years.

The Committee was also to tell management to "give Brodine his contract as assistant principal."

John MacEnulty (tuba) was chair that season. The Committee was broadly representative of most sections and all trends in the orchestra. It included Warren Claunch (bass), Sylvia King (viola), Bob Mottl (assistant principal bassoon), George Silfies (principal clarinet), and Susan Slaughter (trumpet).

The orchestra voted unanimously not to play until the matter was resolved. Even one of the first-chair men who had been looked on as a friend of management said he was tired of being blamed for management's mistakes and voted along with the rest of us.

There had not been such solidarity in the orchestra since the fight against the Van Remoortel dismissal list. Whatever the disagreements on other issues, arbitrary firings or firings for union activity bring unity more quickly and more solidly than almost anything else.

The Committee disappeared in the direction of the Symphony office. The conductor was notified that we were not rehearsing. There was a great feeling of unity and of pride in sticking together and digging our heels in. There was also growing suspense as the minutes and then the hours ticked by.

The lunch break came and went. It was time for the afternoon rehearsal to begin. We were still waiting. Finally, one of the Committee members emerged, waved away questions and got me aside.

"Would you consider a very advantageous early retirement?" he asked.

"I have to have my contract in my hand," was my answer. "I have to be able to accept it and play next season if that's my choice. But . . . "

I thought about the alternative. Even if I got that contract, playing under Susskind was not going to be comfortable. It sounded as if they wanted to get rid of me, which meant they could make it even more uncomfortable.

"Yes," I agreed, "if I have my contract in one hand, and they want to put a good early retirement deal in the other hand, I would consider accepting it."

He returned to the conference. Not long afterward, the Committee brought back the results to the whole orchestra. All three of the dismissals were revoked. I would receive my contract and would have the choice of accepting it or accepting early retirement, conditions to be worked out to my satisfaction with management.

The Committee was applauded. They had done a great job. The whole orchestra deserved applause. They had made an important point, and made it so forcefully that management became much more cautious about dismissals thereafter. There were many subsequent seasons without any firings, and it still remains the case that conductor and Society in St. Louis must have well-substantiated cause before dismissal can be considered.

Personally I felt vindicated and very, very grateful to the bass section, the Committee, and the orchestra.

I received a letter from James Cain, stating, "Contrary to our previous position, outlined in Peter Pastreich's letter of December 13, 1972, we are prepared to offer you the position of Assistant Principal Bass for the 1973-4 season."

However, the early retirement plan worked out with Jim Cain offered me, in addition to the amount of pension to which I would have been entitled in any case, enough to bring the amount up to my current Symphony salary for the years until I reached sixty-five. My medical coverage would be continued for those years as well.

Virginia and I discussed it at length, and I decided to accept it. After all, I had been a professional musician for forty-three years. I could enjoy doing something else, and enjoy five years of that something else at the same salary I would have been receiving in the Symphony.

The end of the symphony season in Powell Hall seemed to wind up my career, but there was still the summer season in Edwardsville. These pop concerts seemed almost anti-climactic. Yet when we reached the final

Looking uncharacteristically elegant

summer concert, and I took my place in the orchestra for the last time, my head was in a whirl. My whole career seemed to be running through my mind, and I could hardly believe it was really coming to a close.

The orchestra was gathering on the stage in the usual way. The audience of seven or eight thousand was filling the big tent and the outdoor amphitheater as I had seen it do so many times. It was hard to believe that this was my last concert. These thoughts were like counterpoint to the music through the first half of the concert.

At the beginning of the second half, I got a great surprise. Mitch Miller, the conductor, faced the audience and announced.

"There is a musician here who is playing his last concert and retiring after tonight. He must be quite a guy, because everybody is talking about him. Let's give Russell Brodine a farewell ovation."

The audience applause was thrilling. Even more thrilling was the participation of the orchestra, which joined in with a foot-stamping enthusiasm that made the stage thunder and shake.

After the concert, my colleagues gathered around to shake hands, wish me well, and tell me I would be missed. To my surprise, one of the leaders of the faction that had most often been in opposition on orchestra matters was most cordial.

"I know I've been pretty sharp with you guys sometimes," I admitted.

"That's when we learned the most," he replied.

We had a little bass section get-together in a restaurant a few days later. My eight colleagues who had done so much for me gave me photos of the whole section, one in a traditional pose, the other standing with our bows upraised. These are still treasured possessions.

Virginia and I responded with a memo in verse:

There are some who like to say—
While walking backward all the way—
"When everything is said and done
I must take care of Number One."
This may be heard in many places
But not from St. Louis contrabasses.
They say, instead, when things get tough,
"If number one is not enough,

St. Louis Symphony Orchestra Bass Section
First row, l to r:
Henry Loew, Terrence Kippenberger, Warren Claunch, Janice Roberts
Second row, l to r:
Robert Maisel, Joseph Kleeman, Russell Brodine, Richard Muehlmann, Donald Martin

They'll hear from two or four or nine.
We'll lay our jobs all on the line."
They stick their necks out altogether
And thus survive the roughest weather
On careful and mature reflection,
This is the VERY GREATEST SECTION.

AFTER THE CONCERTS

I have some regret that I am no longer playing my bass as I did for more than forty years. So I rather like the feeling that there is something of me still in the St. Louis Symphony. I sold my bass to Carolyn White, who replaced me, so my Nardelli bass is still there. Joe Kleeman is still playing my old Mittenwald. Richard Muehlmann uses the bass bow I made.

I look back on those forty years in music with some satisfaction both in the fiddling and in the fighting. I made my share of mistakes, but I think I can say that I made a unique contribution to the fight. Not that I was a charismatic leader. I was never that. I was often a Committee member, only twice its Chairman. Others had more negotiating skills or made other important contributions.

What I had was the dogged persistence, the unwavering commitment that came from my consciousness of myself as a worker, my understanding of the class nature of the struggle, my vision of our fight as part of a much larger fight that could some day win a socialist society of which music would be a part, really belonging to everyone who loves it.

As I have said, I was always a cooperation buff, a gang player, and a collectivist, not an individualist. Upward mobility is said to be the American Dream. That is my dream but not if it means one individual going upward at the expense of others going downward. Upward mobility for all of us together!

In retiring from the orchestra I did not retire from the larger struggle, but that is another story. This is the story of my life in music. In spite of what I have said about collectivism vs. individualism, I do have to admit that I am the central figure in this book, but as we say in the music business, "If you don't toot your own horn, it remains untooten."

Many friends have asked, what about your post-St. Louis musical career? My usual flippant answer has been "I pumped away at that fiddle for more than 40 years. Enough is enough and too much is sufficient!" But there was little chance at age 61 that I would find a position in a major orchestra. Besides, Virginia's career was blossoming and deserved a better shot. As we walked out of the concert hall for the last time, I said to Virginia, "It's your turn, now."

While we had always shared parenting and I had helped with cooking and other household chores, Virginia had carried the main burden. Since my retirement, I have done almost all of the marketing and cooking. This made it possible for her to complete the environmental books she was then writing and to take this belated opportunity to research and write the novel she had always wanted to write. It was eventually published as *Seed of the Fire.*[23]

Retirement gave me more time for two related hobbies I enjoy: woodcarving and repairing wooden artifacts from Africa. The latter came about because a local gallery imported masks and other African art, some of which were created for specific ceremonies and then discarded, so that they reached this country in poor condition. A former colleague, Ed Murphy, was associated with this gallery and offered me the opportunity.

I admired the art and found it satisfying to restore the damage. My connection with the gallery permitted us to acquire some pieces for ourselves, some of which we still enjoy. Others we have donated to the DuSable Museum in Chicago.

Except for the occasional recording, most of the musical notes I have played sounded once and then were gone. It was fun to work on a piece created by an African artist or to do a carving of my own that remained, real and solid, when the work was done.

I especially enjoyed creating some miniature statues of musicians, each with a humorous twist. I have also made many wooden bowls and spoons for our household use or to give to friends or members of the family. Sometimes I have been asked why I don't make more for sale. My answer is that "Wood carving is not economically feasible." I even made a little sign to that effect to display along with some of my work at a craft fair.

I have sometimes said that I have never done anything economically feasible in my life. Either because of that or in spite of it, I am a happy man. I could also be characterized as a tightwad. Saving a few pennies and nickels here and there, I was very surprised when I arrived at my dotage to find that I had quite a lump with which I can now do some nice things for myself and others too.

In retirement I added another hobby, winemaking. Dandelions, elderberries, plums, pears and rhubarb as well as grapes go into my wines.

Russell decided, not for the first time, to carve up some musicians

The principal oboe player the night before his big solo

Playing pool on tour

The Shy Violinist

The long arm of the viola player

Symphony Society lady on a pedestal

The conductor's stabbing baton

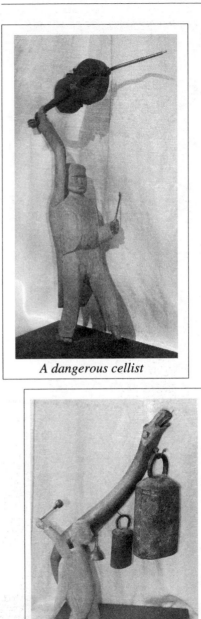

A dangerous cellist

*Fiddle and Fight
on the stand and on the picket line*

Ring my bell

At our surprise 50th wedding anniversary celebration

My lifelong partnership with Virginia continued until her death on May 12, 2000. Her participation in this present work was typically crucial, as was our coalition of over 58 years. Virginia was always a coalition buff. During her very last days, she hoped for enough recovery to be able to take one more crack at bringing the radical movement, labor unions, the environmentalists into closer cooperation. That was not to be. Cancer, which she had battled as part of her environmental program, snatched her from us. We also lost Walter in 1990 and Essie in 1999.

We enjoyed good times with Cynthia and Marc, with Janine and Irv, who have been added to the family by marriage, and with our three granddaughters: Rosario,

Walter in later years

Vonetta, and Francesca Mangaoang-Brodine, and our grandniece Jenny Hughes. It is a comfortable life, free of personal economic worries. That is in part due to our thrifty life style and the rise in real estate prices that made our good-bye to Rocky Branch a re-munerative one. It is much more thanks to social security, won through a struggle led by the unions in the Thirties in which we played our small part, and to the union struggle that brought my pay up in my last years and provided me with a pension.

Rosario, Vonetta and Francesca Mangaoang-Brodine

It did seem that my life in music ended with my retirement, especially since a few years afterward, we moved to Roslyn, a very small town in the Cascade mountains, eighty miles east of Seattle. This removed me even further from the musical world.

However, I began to hear from younger musicians with questions about the past. In response, I was going to write a letter and send some of the documents in my files. When we moved from St. Louis, I had been ready to throw away those files of contracts, programs, letters, clippings, notes, etc. Virginia didn't agree. "That's history," she said.

As I worked at putting some of these papers together, she suggested, "Why not write it up?" So with her help, I wrote a brief paper. We called it "Twenty-four Years of Symphony History: A View From the St. Louis Bass Section."

We sent it to some of my colleagues in St. Louis, to others who had shared that history and were now playing in other orchestras, and to some of the non-musicians who had been so helpful in the 1965 strike. I received some wonderful letters and phone calls in response, and best of all, an invitation from Brad Buckley, one of those colleagues, chairperson of ICSOM, to be keynote speaker at the 1989 ICSOM Conference.

"Twenty-Four Years of Symphony History," was reprinted and distributed to the delegates. (ICSOM conferences are composed of representatives from each of the orchestras and officers of each of the union locals that represent symphony or opera musicians.)

*Some ancient musicians never die, they just wander into
the high mountains in search of Cloud Nine*

It was great to be back among fellow musicians, although in the unusual role of a soloist. The theme of my talk was the theme of my life: unity and solidarity.

I said how thrilled I was with the progress that had been made since I laid down my bass. But I was there to remind them that getting where musicians are today was based on struggle and on unity in that struggle.

"Symphony musicians must work together. The music demands it," I said. "Music comes first even if we don't like the musician sitting on the same stand. That experience has helped us develop unity in struggle. If we don't stay together when we're playing, the music suffers. If we don't stay together in struggles, the union and all its members suffer."

I spoke about the unfinished business of bringing more African-Americans into the orchestras, and of assuring full equality for women.

"Equal opportunity and equal pay for women and for minorities is not a gift white male musicians and union representatives give them. They have had to fight for it and we should fight for it. It is their right. It is in our own interest. Equality means more unity, more dignity and respect for all."

No matter how well we do at the negotiating table on wages and conditions, and as important as they are, I said, "Recognition of our dignity as human beings and as performing artists can't be negotiated. It arises out of standing up for ourselves. It comes from our individual sense that we are not alone, that we have ICSOM and the union behind us."

With the experience of the McCarthy period in mind, I extended the question of unity to musicians with varying political ideas, "If the FBI called musicians Communists, or someone accused them of associating with radicals, they were hounded out of orchestras, out of the union, out of the profession. These people were a loss to the profession and the union. The union suffered further because the threat of being labeled made people afraid to speak up for their rights."

I warned that serious economic recession could threaten our gains, as "experience tells us that in a depression orchestras are among the first to feel the cold wind." In such a case, "we need a strong union more than ever."

I talked about the need for a strong union voice in Washington, D.C. and the need for solidarity against the union busting threat that has existed ever since unions first tried to organize, but that came in with a new virulence and a new power when Reagan broke PATCO, the air traffic controllers union.

I wound up by pointing out that "Sometimes our opposition isn't on the podium, in the manager's office, or across the negotiating table. Today the main opposition is the general corporate offensive against unions."

My talk was received enthusiastically, a rewarding experience for a man who has previously been on stage to speak only through the music of his instrument.

Senza Sordino, the name of the ICSOM newsletter could almost have been my lifelong slogan, as I said at the conference, because I've been talking and working for unionism all my life, although at times I had to speak *soto voce*.

I thought my ICSOM conference speech was my last shot at trying to help improve my beloved profession, but here I am again, with this book, speaking *senza sordino*.[24]

I still say, as I did there, "We learned the hard way that though we do our work in white tie and tails, we have to struggle for better pay and conditions just like those who work in blue collars and jeans. We need the labor movement and it needs us. That's the basis of solidarity."

NOTES AND REFERENCES

1.   Edward W. Arian, *Bach, Beethoven and Bureaucracy: The Case of the Philadelphia Orchestra* (University of Alabama Press, University, Alabama, 1971).

2.   Esther W. Campbell, *Bagpipes in the Wind Section, A History of the Seattle Symphony and its Women's Association* (Seattle Symphony Women's Association, Seattle, Washington, 1978).

3.   James P. Kraft, "The 'Pit' Musicians: Mechanization in the Movie Theater, 1926-1934," *Labor History* 35:66, Winter, 1994.

4.   In 1933, the Roosevelt administration proposed and Congress passed the National Industrial Recovery Act. Section 7A of this Act stated that "employees have the right to organize and bargain collectively through representatives of their own choosing, and shall be free from the interference, restraint or coercion of employers of labor or their agents." Although the Supreme Court declared the NIRA unconstitutional two years later, the right to organize was almost immediately embodied in the Wagner Labor Relations Act.

5.   Herbert Biberman, *Salt of the Earth* (Beacon Press, Boston, 1965), pp. 141-146.

6.   Ann Fagan Ginger and David Christiano, *The Cold War Against Labor* (2 vols. Meiklejohn Civil Liberties Institute, Berkeley, California, 1987).

7.   *Bach, Beethoven and Bureaucracy* and Edward W. Arian, *The Unfulfilled Promise, Public Subsidy of the Arts.*

8.   *Senza Sordino*, 31, No. 1, October 1992.

9.   Katherine Hepburn, *Me: Stories of My Life* (Knopf, New York, 1990), p. 214.

10.   Katherine Gladney Wells, *Symphony and Song* (The Countryman Press, St. Louis, 1980), p. 69.

11.   George Seltzer, *Music Matters* (The Scarecrow Press, Inc., Metuchen, New Jersey and London, 1989), p. 9.

12.   Beatrice Lumpkin, *Always Bring a Crowd: The Story of Frank Lumpkin, Steelworker* (International Publishers, New York, 1999).

13.   Tom Hall, "The First 25 Years of the International Conference of Symphony and Opera Musicians," paper prepared for the 25th annual meeting of ICSOM in 1987.

14. Wells, p. 5.

15. "Dispute Over Symphony Firings," *St. Louis Post-Dispatch*, March 2, 1959.

16. Wells, p.5.

17. Selzer, pp. 1-10.

18. Chuck Finney's "Blue Notes," *St. Louis Argus* (date uncertain, probably 1960).

19. William Schatzkamer, personal communication.

20. Selzer, p. 112

21. Martin Goldsmith, *The Inextinguishable Symphony* (John Wiley & Sons, Inc., New York, 2000).

22. Press release issued by Anita L. Bond and Ruth C. Porter, November 22, 1963.

23. Virginia Warner Brodine, *Seed of the Fire* (International Publishers, New York, 1996).

24. Russell and Virginia Warner Brodine's papers are deposited in the Lewis J. Ort Library at Frostburg State University, Frostburg, Maryland.

Appendix
The 1958 St. Louis Survey

The first known survey of wages and working conditions in orchestras was done by the AFM in 1952. (That survey was published in Senza Sordino, Vol. XV, No. 4, April 1977) However, the earliest and most comprehensive survey done by musicians themselves before the formation of ICSOM was undertaken in 1958 by the St. Louis Symphony Orchestra Committee. The survey project was spearheaded by Edward Ormond, Chairman, with Russell Brodine and Henry Loew (who became the St. Louis Symphony's first ICSOM delegate). The St. Louis Committee issued a report to the orchestras that participated in the survey, which contained a tabulation of the statistics gathered along with some prescient questions and conclusions.

The St. Louis Symphony Orchestra Committee (Local 2 AFM) wishes to thank all the individual musicians and orchestra committees who responded to our questionnaire and thereby made this report possible. Having the information compiled here has already been helpful to us in preparing contract proposals for next year and presenting our case to management. We hope it will be similarly helpful to other orchestras. It was gratifying to receive answers from other cities which were not only complete and interesting, but expressive of enthusiasm for the idea of inter-orchestra communications and further cooperation. The following quotes are samples of the comments received:

Excellent idea—Great need for clarification of working conditions and establishing liaison . . . . Your problems are our problems. . . . The problems of the symphony musician must be brought to the attention of members of Congress, public, etc. . . .Perhaps it would be a good idea to have a sort of linkage between us all. . . .I will discuss with him (AFM President Herman Kenin) the possibility of setting up a sort of convention for symphony players.

The picture presented by this survey is not a pretty one for the performing musicians. It is not too much to say that it indicates the existence of a real crisis in the symphony field. As we have gone over the conditions existing in one city after another, it seems to us that these answers raise many new questions. How should musicians seek to better present their situation? Through our union, of course—certainly more regular, active participation in our locals, closer cooperation of orchestra personnel, orchestra committees and union officers is a basic necessity if any gains are to be made. But can each individual AFM local solve each orchestra situation in isolation? Isn't a broader approach necessary? What about the proposal contained in more than one reply, that our International Union sponsor a symphony conference?

Should we take a more direct interest in the question of how symphony orchestras are supported financially? Is the current crisis due to an outmoded system of obtaining support for our orchestras? If so, what other sources could be tapped? Is municipal, state or federal subsidy the answer? Is reaching a wider segment of the public the answer? Or should we merely press our demands determinedly upon the present Symphony Associations and let them solve the problem of finding the necessary funds?

We believe that music is a vital part of our culture, and that it is possible for it to play an increasingly important role in the lives of the American people. But the possibility of growth and development, even the present status of music, is threatened by the economic insecurity of our jobs and the almost total lack of respect and prestige connected with our profession.

It is our hope that this report will make a small contribution to furthering discussion and action toward the improvement of the performing musicians' income, security and status and the revitalization of our country's musical life.

Notes for chart on page 178
* under negotiation
** at the time of the survey, participation in Social Security was voluntary for non-profit organizations.

Orchestra	Winter weeks	min. weekly salary	automatic raises?	Unempl. ins.?	Social Sec?	Health ins.	pension?	summer season?	summer seaon length	summer salary	paid vacation?	tour length	transport.	per diem	ratify contract?	dismissal ctte.?	metro area pop.
Met Opera	31.5	$166.95	no	yes	yes	no	no	no			no	7	rr	$10.25	yes	yes	8,142,000
NY Phil	32	$157.50	no	yes	yes	no	yes	yes	6	$140	yes	none	rr-bus	$12	yes	yes	8,142,000
Chicago	30	$155	no	no	yes	no	yes	yes	6	$125	no	varies	rr-air	$12.50	no	yes	6,300,000
Los Angeles	24	$121	no	yes	yes	no	*	yes	8	$121	no	one-nighter	bus	$11	yes	yes	5,572,124
Boston	40	$140	no	no	yes	yes	yes	yes	6	$140	no	5	rr	$14	yes	yes	3,141,623
Philadelphia	32	$157.50	no	yes	yes	yes	yes	yes	6	$132.50	no	4	rr	$13	no	no	2,180,300
Cleveland	31	$130	no	yes	yes	no	yes	yes	8	$84	no	4	rr-bus	$13	no	no	2,000,000
Detroit	25	$120	no	yes	yes	yes	*	yes	12	$70	no	5	rr-air	$10	no	yes	1,912,000
St. Louis	25	$105	no	*	yes	no	*	no			no	3	bus	$10	no	yes	1,892,000
San Francisco	22	$120	no	no	yes	no	yes	yes	10	$46	no	none			yes	yes	1,721,170
Buffalo	23	$100	no	yes	yes	no	no	yes	8	$19	no	none			no	yes	1,653,363
Pittsburgh	27	$125	no	yes	yes	no	no	no			no	5	bus	$12	no	yes	1,601,700
Cincinnati	28	$112.50	no	no	yes	no	yes	no			no	3	rr-bus	$12	no	yes	1,514,000
Dallas	23	$90	yes	no	yes	no	*	no			no	none	rr-bus	$10.50	no	yes	1,415,400
Indianapolis	22	$80	yes	no	yes	no	no	no			no	1 to 3	bus	$10	no	no	1,272,700
Minneapolis	27	$110	no	yes	yes	no	no	no			no	8	rr-bus	$11	no	no	1,215,000
Kansas City	20	$85	no	no	yes	no	no	no			no	none			no	no	1,191,000
New Orleans	25	$95	no	no	yes	no	no	no	yes	4	$70	no	4.5	bus	$4.50	no	yes	1,123,640
Denver	20	$70	no	no	yes	no	no	no			$70	no	1	bus	$9	no	no	877,933
Rochester	30	$110	no	*	yes	no	no	no				no	none		$10	no	no,	772,971

Index